finding
magic in
the mess

finding magic in the mess

A Path to Greater Presence and More Joy,
One Parenting Moment at a Time

Dr. Steven Fonso, B.Sc., D.C.

A TARCHERPERIGEE BOOK

tarcherperigee

An imprint of Penguin Random House LLC
penguinrandomhouse.com

Library of Congress Cataloging-in-Publication Data

Names: Fonso, Steven, author.
Title: Finding magic in the mess : a path to greater presence
and more joy, one parenting moment at a time / Steven Fonso.
Description: New York : TarcherPerigee, 2019.
Identifiers: LCCN 2019005257| ISBN 9780525541561 (hardback) |
ISBN 9780525504887 (ebook)
Subjects: LCSH: Parenting. | Parent and child. | Families. |
BISAC: FAMILY & RELATIONSHIPS / Parenting / Motherhood. |
FAMILY & RELATIONSHIPS / Life Stages / School Age. |
BODY, MIND & SPIRIT / Meditation.
Classification: LCC HQ755.8 .F646 2019 | DDC 306.874—dc23
LC record available at https://lccn.loc.gov/2019005257
p.   cm.

Printed in the United States of America
1   3   5   7   9   10   8   6   4   2

Book design by Laura K. Corless

To my beautiful wife, Lea, for her endless support each and every day, and her relentless commitment to our vision for our family and beyond . . . so much love and gratitude that you are in my life.

To my children, Maiah, Logan, and Hannah, for being such fun-loving souls to play with every day, teaching me all about surrendering, and for the gift of watching you explore the world from a parent's perspective.

The universe is not one of individual things,
but rather one of process, a changing, flowing, evolving,
and intimately interconnected system of interactions.
It is not of the flow, it is the flow.

—AUTHOR UNKNOWN

contents

1

THE DAILY GRIND
The Suffering Is Real

2

WAKING

Opening Ourselves to a New Way

3

PRACTICE

Parenting in the Moment, Day by Day

TRANSFORM
The Journey Continues

foreword

You are about to read a book that will change how you view parenting—information that will surely improve your parenting skills and increase your parenting joy. Some might refer to *Finding Magic in the Mess* as brilliant. I would agree. It will provide you with easy-to-understand principles and strategies to manage your life. Some might refer to this as a book that everyone should read. I would agree with that statement as well. Some books are written for quick review. Others should be studied in depth, and this is one of the latter for sure. I have known Dr. Steven Fonso for more than a decade, and I have watched him develop into a wonderfully talented doctor, husband, and father. He has embarked on the teaching of one of the most important and life-affecting subjects—raising a human being.

What would your life as a parent be like if you knew how to preset your almost automatic response mechanism in such a way that you would remain calm and poised, no matter what issue you face, no matter the age of your child? Most parents desire to improve their parenting skills, but they are often lost. They live a life filled with questions and doubt and rarely know where to turn for answers. Most of us recognize that parenting is all about "on the job" training, and we have no trainer; it's difficult to find clear processes that can put the growth puzzle together. Now you no longer need to be searching. The answers to so many of the most common parenting challenges are addressed in this book.

Yet the most important part of this information is contained in the questions you read and the actions you will take. The insights offered, the simplicity and eloquence of the words espoused, and the challenges discussed, are all there for you to grasp, understand, and implement to achieve a more joyful and exciting parenting experience, while raising children who discover peace and love, and who love to explore the magnificence they are.

From this moment forward, as you read the following pages with diligence, think of how you can immediately apply what you have learned to shift how you think, feel, respond, and perform as a parent. You are in for a wonderful experience. Your children will be the grateful recipients of this new learning.

The world needed a book like this, and now it has arrived. Well done.

—Dr. Gilles LaMarche,
author, international speaker, and educator

finding
magic in
the mess

introduction

Choosing to Transform from Stressed to Present

Twelve years ago I became a parent. You know what happens next: Your whole world cracks open. You see the world through the eyes of a parent. You actually start seeing kids where you didn't before: the malls, grocery stores, and restaurants. You are now part of this "club." Everything just changes.

Everything also changed in my practice. With more than 115,000 office visits to date, I've had the privilege of working as a hands-on holistic chiropractor for the past fifteen years. I have a unique skill set to be able to feel the spinal tension and relate that to how people are handling the stress in their life. And what I began to notice now that I was in the parent club was how the restless sleeps, the worries, concerns, and fears for their kids were affecting the health of these parents in my practice. I also observed that when parents adopted a more flexible and lighthearted view of parenting, their health was not impacted as drastically: they conserved more energy, had more resilience, and overall enjoyed a better parenting experience. And since I was trained in body, mind, and spirit practices, the level of health on all these dimensions was interesting to me not only as a parent but also clinically, as a doctor.

As I dived into my work years ago, I was aware that my personal values are spirituality, personal development, family, and health, and because of this, I've been blessed to place myself in front of some of the top healers, thinkers, and health crusaders in the world today. And when you put your hand in a jar of glue, you can't help but some of it sticking—these men and women have been a massive influence over the years to teach me about human behavior, psychosomatic (body-mind) healing, holistic health, family dynamics, relationships, and consciousness—both from the Far East to the Far West. I don't necessarily choose specific teachers; I feel they fall into my lap depending on what I'm ready to hear. I tend to take an insight and an idea, meditate on it, and then weave it into my daily life. After nearly twenty years of clinical practice, studying, meditating, and gaining life experiences, a self-awareness guide for parents—*Finding Magic in the Mess*—came to life.

As time went on and our kids began to get a little older, I was able to better understand the stress in our home and how much of it we were creating for no reason at all. After some deep reflection and even some quality meditative time away from the pressures of the daily grind, I began to collect my thoughts on this newfound perspective, along with some heart-centered solutions for myself as well as for other parents who were struggling unnecessarily. I hadn't planned on writing a book for parents, but lo and behold, solutions came through—and here they are. In addition to transforming my life as a parent, these insights have also added a new dimension to my practice, through well-attended workshops, community outreach, and more meaningful changes in individual patients' outlook than I can count. With this book, I hope you'll take this journey with me too—not in person, but just as powerfully nonetheless.

This book is about a new way of being—a new way of relating to yourself and with your family. It presents a paradigm and lifestyle that encourages parents to adopt a fresh approach, a new set of standards if you will, that when applied will produce meaningful if not magical results for both you and your family. The power of the material is in both the contemplation and application. When you create space in your day to ask essential questions and then apply your insights, transformation will come your way. Some of the ideas in the pages that follow might seem counterintuitive, or simply different from what you've always believed. Play with them. Experiment. With an open mind and heart, explore which ones feel useful for you on your parenting journey.

Admittedly, there was no catastrophic event in my life or personal tragedy prompting me to share these ideas. I did, though, have a sudden epiphany nudging me to put pen to paper. The inspiration was my patients who were parents without solutions, stressed without awareness, and trapped in the merry-go-round of life, feeling unfulfilled. I knew these challenges are universal, and if they were having them, others were as well.

So I took my keen interest in questioning the nature of reality, who we are, and what we do in our day-to-day life as people and started writing. I watched and listened each day as my wife and I went through the throes of everyday life. I questioned our culture, the rules, the values, our stresses, and our inner experience of well-being.

With that, I noticed how we as parents were susceptible to getting trapped within the cultural norms, ideals, and standards set forth by our parents, grandparents, and others who had a part in raising us.

I noticed what was stressful, confusing, incongruent, or creating discontent within us. We began to break some of these beliefs, ideals, expectations, and illusions within ourselves. I observed what were mindless thoughts or actions or consistent struggles, as well as some new perspectives that were needed to transcend our everyday challenges.

My idea was to become more aware and empowered within ourselves. As I documented our own solutions, I noticed patients in my private practice needing these same insights and solutions.

And so all of that culminated in creating this book, so my wife and I can create a new "point of focus" together that will give parents, partners, and spouses permission to go further in their relationships and live exceptionally—for the sake of ourselves and our kids.

control and surrender

As a practicing holistic doctor, husband, and father, I have been fascinated with the idea that we are spiritual beings having a physical experience. I have been studying consciousness and culture for almost two decades and was amazed at how these studies began to apply directly to my role as a parent. I have been blessed to be involved in attending and creating programs that have provided me access to insights and energy that is often difficult to find in everyday life.

As I began to delve deeper into my experience as a human being, and as a spouse and parent, it became clear that one glaring pair of opposites continued to surface time and time again in my daily life: control and surrender.

I've chosen to become more self-aware—to see this amazing dance between chasing that which I didn't have or clinging to that which I did have (control), and allowing everything to be just as it was in that moment (surrender).

Every time I observed that I was in fear and stress, I was attempting to control something. Every time I felt love and gratitude, I was in a state of accepting everything as it was—a state of surrender. When I surrendered to life as it was, there was such a richer experience and range of feeling— more flexibility and ease in my body, more laughter, lightness, happiness, and joy. When I was attempting to control my wife's thoughts, or my kids' actions, I would shift to a state of rigidity—"high alert"— and a place of tension, frustration, anger, or irritation. I would lose touch with my internal rhythms and cues. The more awareness I brought to this control and surrender thing, the more I realized how the culture that I had been brought up in was all about trying to control everyone and everything around me. This had me quite intrigued.

We have been conditioned to be control freaks.

Although this bouncing back and forth from control to surrender had me feeling slightly unstable, it allowed me to observe the relevance and implications for myself as well as society's health and well-being. I realize we have been conditioned to be control freaks.

This was a great epiphany, providing me with tremendous fuel for transformation. It was time to break the rules of control and embrace surrender instead.

Surrender did not mean turning over responsibility for my life, nor did it mean to be passive with low standards. It did not mean weakness, less than, or submissive. In fact, it was quite the opposite.

Surrendering brought me to be fully present with what was going on, taking full responsibility and accountability, and make more fully aware choices. When I was in a state of surrender, I felt present, focused, more flexible and adaptable in daily challenges. I was able to make more authentic, productive, and pro-

As you surrender, gressive choices for myself and my family.

you gain presence. The experiences and growing awareness allowed me to further gain insights as to how we as parents can better maximize our precious time with our families.

Since most of humanity hangs in the control state, as you surrender, you gain presence, and as you do this, you simultaneously begin to awaken. You become available to the magic of unlimited energy, insights, intuition, and inspiration. You see things as they really are.

For most of us, surrendering means breaking new ground. This can be uncomfortable. Most growth has a level of discomfort within it. In the unwinding, it forces the body-mind to leave the comfort zone, and stretches or even dissolves your ideas, beliefs, and rules you have developed about relationships, kids, and life.

Throughout this book I present daily experiences and opportunities to go deeper, accessing a heightened level of awareness to evaluate your thoughts, emotions, and behaviors. The suggested ideas, questions, and insights are tools to assist you in exploring why you are doing what you are doing.

The book is not so much about beliefs and rules. Rather, it is about self-inquiry and self-discovery. The idea is to create a pause in your habitual way of being so that you can access a new level of relationship with yourself and your family. It's not necessarily about making life easier; it's about a deeper level of awareness and more rich and present experience with life and the people around you.

how to use this book

Whether reading this book front to back or jumping from topic to topic, simply observe your reactions for what they are and see the colorful shifts in your perspectives and awareness that will unfold for you. My intention is that the concepts we cover together challenge, inspire, liberate, and awaken you to a new and healthier version of yourself, and that simultaneously you grow in your relationships with your family and children. Is there anything more important to the future of the planet than helping the next generation be healthy, living authentically, and congruent to their core nature and core values, while living in love and appreciation for inclusiveness, celebrating the diversity and uniqueness of one another?

At the end of each section you'll find one or more questions for reflection. I encourage you to pause and let them percolate. If you keep a journal, these would be great questions to write your thoughts about. If not, simply hold them in your mind and let your own answers rise to the surface. The more you make space for this type of inquiry, the more present you'll find yourself becoming. In place of a specific workbook, I was inspired to provide you with elevating your awareness through specific "affirmations" to support you in your ongoing journey through parenting. These mantras are designed to introduce specific thought patterns in different circumstances and situations. They provide and encourage trust, reflection, expansion, flow, and ease through difficulties and reinforce what you already know to be true.

Parenting is a spiritual game of waking up. It takes what you think you know, who you think you are, your rules on life, your values, your routines, and shatters it all, leaving you with a blank canvas to create the new you.

The question is, will you make yourself receptive for this transformation?

May you enjoy the surrendering of each and every moment,
DR. STEVEN FONSO

1

the daily grind

The Suffering Is Real

suf·fer·ing

the state of undergoing pain, distress, or hardship

It seems fitting to start the conversation with a topic that so many of us attempt to avoid. No one wants to admit it, but we all suffer. At times, each of us feels helpless, powerless, and overwhelmed. Bedtime, laundry, dishes, cleaning, putting away toys, brushing teeth, screaming, yelling, fighting, and more. When is this going to end? Sometimes it feels like nothing works.

This is part of the human experience that is so difficult for us as parents to acknowledge or accept. We try our best to put on a smile and hold it all together, and inside, we are feeling frazzled, disconnected, or unfulfilled.

Suffering is one of those things that may fly under the radar for quite some time. It is not always obvious, particularly because we're trying so hard to tune it out. So part of us needs to connect with and uncover the aspects of parenting that we may be blind to in the midst of our own suffering.

What I do know is that when we genuinely acknowledge and accept our suffering just as it is, just as we are experiencing it, we can be liberated. Without doing so, we stay stuck in the loop of endless trying, frustration, and judgment. Staying in stress is not where we want to be. Let's connect with suffering so that we can move on and awaken our authentic greatness.

what disconnection looks like

You lay your head on the pillow after an exhausting, action-packed day. As you lie there, there is an inner sense of dissatisfaction. You are feeling the pressures of not enough time in the day, worrying about things that are out of your control, and wondering if the busyness is ever going to end.

All this mental chatter consumes you as you make a feeble attempt to quiet your mind. You feel you have done all you can do yet still feel a sense of disconnection within yourself, your partner, and your kids. You feel that there is something missing, and there must be more, but you can't quite put your finger on it. Is this all there is to life? This is suffering.

You may also be a parent who feels you need to work all the time, that there is always something you have to do. You feel that your kids need to be involved in every possible activity, and there may be a consistent and low-grade feel of angst within the household. This is suffering.

You may be the parent who attempts to exemplify that you are a family where everything is perfect, life is always wonderful, you personify perfection as a family, that your family is perpetually in a state of bliss and wonder and awe for every blade of grass you come across. You inflate how wonderful every single day is, as it goes off without a hitch. This is suffering.

The suffering parent is the version of you that will always think there is not enough; you don't have enough energy to make it through the day, you don't have enough money to buy what you want, you aren't doing enough to raise a happy family, you don't know enough to make the right choices, the kids aren't having enough experiences, they aren't smart enough or perfect enough and you don't have enough time to get all the things done that you need to do.

For these voids of not enough, you deflate or inflate reality in an attempt to avoid your suffering. You burn out or burn up inside.

Through the hazy eyes of the suffering parent, we will never be quite good enough to meet the expectations and standards that our culture places on us.

We are shown through the internet, magazines, and media what it looks like to have the perfect family, and within our suffering, we always feel as though we fall short of meeting those standards. As we ebb and flow through life, we are all going to take on the role of the disconnected parent at one point or another. Now would be a great time to take a look at yourself and your family. Connect with and appreciate the life you have right now, at this point. Look at the faces in your mind, hold their image: the innocence, the beauty, the love.

If you place your hands over your heart, can you feel the rhythms of ease and connection as you breathe slowly and gently in and out?

the dangling carrots

know there is pressure that society places on you. I've felt it time and time again. There are unrealistic expectations placed on the family to make sure that your children get all the experiences they need to make it in this world. It can be horribly stressful, can't it? Not only the stresses of whether you are doing things right but also how the heck you manage your thoughts and emotions in the face of loud, busy, and often chaotic days.

At the end of the day, society and culture impose a tremendous number of ideals on us as individuals and as parents. The media reinforces what success, happiness, and fulfillment look like. They are the three dangling carrots of *make more, buy more,* and *do more.* They tell you how life should play out for you and your family.

As we try so desperately to swim upstream, to meet these expectations, we base our success or failure on them, we exhaust ourselves physically, emotionally, and mentally. We sacrifice our well-being, losing touch with the core essence of who we and our children truly are.

Waking up from the suffering mind helps us to connect to what is really important, especially in a culture of 1,001 choices and comparing yourself to everyone else's beautifully painted life.

Having worked with thousands of people to help them transform their lives and revitalize their health and well-being, I assure you that the pressures you place on yourself are not only unnecessary but also damaging to your body, heart, mind, and family.

Wouldn't it be great if you could find greater depth in everyday life that would transform your stresses into joy, your frustrations into laughter, and your suffering into unwavering love and gratitude?

This is all possible, but you must first wake from the suffering mind.

What are the dangling carrots in which you define your success, happiness, or fulfillment as a parent and family?

the chasing game

nside you, "chasing" the carrots shows up in different forms. It may be experienced through a chatty mind that won't turn off; or feel like tension in your body, neck, or spine; or your body becomes symptomatic with digestive problems, anxious or depressive states. Your brain goes into overdrive with your foot cranked on the gas pedal, spinning the tires while feeling the churning on the inside. Anger, discontentment, and frustration are all signs of chasing that which you can't quite attain.

You may be chasing more time, more money, and more stuff and often striving to gain a false sense of control from that which you feel powerless. Your body-mind is giving you feedback to stop chasing and become present; to surrender and to tune in to yourself.

You know what will make you content in your heart, yet this contentment often eludes you. No amount of chasing will provide the fulfillment you're craving within or transform you into a peaceful being.

Fulfillment comes from the inside and cannot be attained from the outside. This inside-out approach to fulfillment is the complete opposite thinking, and a departure from, the cultural epidemic of thinking fulfillment comes from sources outside of you.

Now, as humanity shifts into more awakened consciousness and more awareness, we draw the magnifying glass closer to what is really going on. The game of life changes. As the game naturally changes, so do our thoughts, emotions, actions, and consequences.

Where does society have you hooked?

What do you consistently chase?

Who does that really serve?

stress equals fear

Although stress is an important growth factor for all people, most of today's "distress" is a direct result of fear. If you live a life of trying to match the Joneses, where you attempt to fit into societal standards, you will feel the pressure of the external stress and the fear of expectations that you place on yourself to fit into this mold; back to the "chasing game" again.

We often do things in our daily life out of a place of fear, to gain acceptance, love, and approval from our family and peers. When we try to live by someone else's standards, we will fear that we don't have enough time, energy, or resources to meet those expectations. This is why we lie in bed at night with a mind that won't turn off.

When we feel stress, this potentially indicates that we are not living *our* lives, but trying to live the ideals and values of someone else. Isn't this the opposite of what we know to be true? Each of us, including our children, are individuals, with different needs, yet we ignore that within ourselves and try to fit into the mold of what everyone else is doing.

If we live a life of authenticity, where we are inspired from within and we set our own standards of living, which is honoring each individual as unique, we rest our head quietly at night knowing that all is well.

What areas of your life seem to be ruled by stress?

Where is the fear coming from?

Whose standards are you trying to live up to?

the unconscious mind

Right or wrong? Should I or shouldn't I? Have you ever used these words while making a decision for your kids?

The unconscious mind is a powerful place most people make decisions from, and they don't realize what is really happening. This type of decision-making is similar to when you have reached your destination while driving your vehicle and wonder how you even got there.

While you were driving, your conscious mind went somewhere else. A different part, your subconscious mind, drove the vehicle perfectly based on old programming. You can't believe you drove through four green lights and made two right turns to get there, but you did, all without consciously thinking.

Much like driving your vehicle unconsciously, we often make decisions that come from the unconscious mind: the mind of a preprogrammed person. When you are using phrases like "I should" or "I ought to," or "I'm supposed to," you are not making conscious choices.

These are preprogrammed rules you are abiding by from someone in your past. Those unconscious parts of you that have been trained by others are making your decisions for you and your kids; instead of your own conscious awareness.

Right or wrong, "should or shouldn't" is made up of others' values and stems from a core of fear. This line of questioning creates stress because you are not bringing your full awareness in the moment to make the choice for what is happening right now, in the present. You attempt to make a decision from a belief you were taught from someone else's belief system, instead of listening to your own heart.

When you choose from the unconscious mind, you will try to avoid the pain of being wrong and being a failure as well as the pleasure of being accepted and being loved.

An interesting observation is if you want to get to work and back or drive to a familiar spot, going on autopilot and tuning out will still get you there. If you want to go somewhere new, somewhere you haven't been before, you must drive with a conscious mind and a high awareness for the choices you are making and the turns you need to make.

When you are going somewhere new, your inner voice sounds so different. You are present and aware.

When you are going somewhere new, your inner voice sounds so different. You are present and aware.

This also holds true for parenting. If you want a new destination for your kids, different from that of you or your parents, more conscious awareness of your choices is required. This is the reason it is so essential to spend time really getting to know your inner values and your vision for your family.

Parents who are in tune with their highest versions of themselves create a great deal of internal contentment because they are not being swayed in their decisions. The clarity and vision for their children is crystal clear. Their decisions are coming from a place of authenticity, ease, and love.

When do you frequently go on autopilot?

What are a few decisions you are working on that require more heart-centered attentiveness?

where is the fun?

Remember when you were a little kid and you were along for the ride—you just lived for the moment and experienced life with joy, excitement, and anticipation? Nothing was too difficult, too draining, too time-consuming, or overly pressured. There was just a "going with the flow."

That is the pure, innocent child: a part of you that never dies. And then you spend a good portion of your life ignoring this essence and burying your head into adulthood, with the rules and conditions that come with being one.

What if you tapped into your inner child just like that little free spirit you once were? Do you remember who that kid was? The part of you that doesn't overthink but just loves the ride and loves being alive? The one who gives big smiles just for the sake of smiling? The one who jumps puddles just for the sake of jumping puddles? To see the world unfiltered and connected. To embrace that part of you that is curious about everything. This is the playful version of you we are inviting to come out.

*How can you embrace your inner child
and elevate the amount of curiosity in your day?*

*How can you amplify the amount of fun
you experience in your relationships?*

ask yourself why

"hy am I saying no to my kids?"

"Why did I answer their question so fast?"

"Why am I not letting them do something they are asking?"

The question of asking yourself "why" is a great way to interrupt your usual, knee-jerk patterns. This will generate a pattern interrupt within your normal decision-making process. Immediately when you ask why, your higher brain centers light up.

Your mind sharpens its focus into the present moment like a car honking brings your conscious mind's focus on the road. You instantly become aware as soon as you realize you are not aware. You begin to become aware of the autopilot, unconscious you.

Anytime you ask the question why, you stop the habitual, mindless behavior and you enter into a space of inquiry for greater depth of clarity. This question may have to be asked many times, as your initial response may be to answer the question very quickly. By asking why, you can start the process of deconstructing your automatic beliefs, thoughts, and actions and get to a new level of awareness as to what is really running your decisions.

In the shower one day, I picked up my razor to shave and I asked the simple question, "Why am I going to shave right now?" I came up with about eight reasons, and most of them were from stories that I had picked up over time. The stories ranged from looking more professional, being liked, looking honest, et cetera. If these rules were determining my behavior with a swipe of my razor blade, could you imagine how many stories are running our lives, our decisions, and our actions?

Realizing that parts of you have been hooked by the shoulds and should-nots of parenting is always a humbling experience. Breaking the habit of being you will be the biggest challenge facing a more aware parent.

It's easy to stay the same, and it's challenging to ask yourself new questions. We start with the question of "why." If you want to live an authentic, independent, and liberated life, you must ask yourself why.

Why would you want to become a more aware parent?

What areas of parenting need more "why" questions?

Asking "why" takes some discipline because we aren't used to asking it. By asking the question though, you have a moment of surrendering and you instantly create a more clear mind-heart connection.

The process of asking why is what I call "confusion to clarity." You confuse or mix up your normal patterning and allow a new level of organization to ensue. You allow an immediate introspective, unwinding, and discarding process that allows you to truly become more congruent with your core nature.

You are a combination of your life experiences and have developed hardwired habits to this point. Your body-mind ravels together tensions, postures, beliefs, values, responses, reactions, and emotions that combine to form your personality.

If you are to go to another level of living, then you need to be open to throwing all those on the table and let yourself be vulnerable to growth. Take the current puzzle that is you, smash it on the ground, and gently move the magnifying lens closer on each of the pieces.

After asking the question of "why" to magnify clarity for your routines and behaviors, you begin to drop control and surrender to the moment. This brings presence.

Surrendering into presence is being and living your life in greater awareness, seeing and feeling connection to life, observing order and synchronicity in your family, environment, and world.

Most parents today were raised in a culture of plow forward, domination, hierarchy, and authority; don't question the doctor, kids know nothing, parents rule the kids, be obedient and submissive to authority, do what you are told, et cetera.

We had not been shown to ask high-quality questions. By adding new questions into your day, you create the opportunity to discover where your decisions for yourself and your family are really coming from.

We all want the best for our families and to live according to our highest values. To achieve this, we sometimes have to break free from the way we were taught and raised. We have to forge our own path.

In order to guide our children to live authentically and follow their dreams, we first need to be living this way ourselves.

Can you ask a partner, friend, or close relative where they feel you could use more awareness with respect to your relationship with your child?

tuning in to your essence

I f asking why begins to break your unconscious patterning, then what takes place after that?

Being conscious.

What is being conscious then? Being conscious is having our most evolved portions of our brain activated and tuned in to our heart. This produces massive new levels of awareness that can allow us to lead our lives more authentically. We no longer are functioning from the most primitive parts of the unconscious mind, but with a brain-heart connection, we access more aware states of consciousness.

Moving from a fear-based unconscious mind to a love-based, heart-centered awareness allows us to tap into our true essence.

Pause and breathe. Breathe in through your mouth and out your nose. Feel the rise and fall of your belly as you do this a few times. To sense your essence, you focus on the moment and get present.

As you consciously breathe in this moment, your essence cares not of rules, image, personality, culture, or identity. Your essence is here for the experience of wholeness, and part of this journey is waking ourselves to each new level of awareness. Essence equals awareness. Awareness equals presence. Presence equals connection. Connection equals love.

What if tuning in to your essence was the point of parenting? What if this was your baseline for living? How would you speak, act, and think from this place of awareness? What if you decided not to do what the culture dictates is right or wrong, or what you were raised to believe, but you began to bypass those things and started listening to and following your waking self?

How would your children benefit from a parent who lives his or her life from this heightened space of heart-centered awareness?

When you truly feel connected, what do you tend to focus on?
Do you focus on the mess or do you focus on the magical opportunities?

our kids are here to assist

Fortunately, we won't be alone in this venture. Our kids are here to help us. They will expose the parts of us that go on autopilot throughout the day, those versions of us that just lose it, snap, rage (it's okay, we all do it); that give little awareness to what we are doing, thinking, or feeling; this part of us that functions in a low state of awareness.

Our kids will help us wake up. They will help access those parts of us that we deny, repress, or ignore. Don't like anger? They will bring that part out! Don't like weakness? They will expose that part. Don't like selfishness? They will help you access that too.

The beauty of the family matrix is the intermingling of the various energies to create wholeness. The chaotic times are there assisting us to organize to greater levels of awareness.

If we want to go deeper in our journey, then gone are the days where we mindlessly regurgitate what our grandparents or parents taught without giving it a second thought. Passing down ideas without seeing the bigger or clearer picture is no longer an option.

If we are to have greater influence, we are called to have greater awareness of who we are and how we behave throughout each day, and our kids are just the ones to nudge us forward. Many of us suffer, feel hopeless, angry, frustrated, irritated that our life is not going the way we envisioned. Family is part of our wholeness journey, not there to simply keep us comfortable.

Our kids force us to be present, to be in the moment, to put things into perspective, and to remind us of what's important.

Can you see how both you and your children push each other's buttons to reveal those parts that need more love and acceptance?

Identify one trait that bothers you about your child, and think back to when you were a kid doing the same thing. Why were you doing it? What was the benefit to you?

2

waking

Opening Ourselves to a New Way

wak·ing

**marked by full consciousness, awareness, alertness;
a state of being awake**

Think of awakening or waking up simply as a coming into awareness. For many, waking up may be a new concept. In fact, most people don't even know they are unaware or "asleep" in the first place.

For many these days, the norm is living a fast-paced, high-strung, wound-up, high-pressure life. These are the conditions of the culture that are being set for you, and very often, you will find yourself succumbing to the conditioning.

Often you live the merry-go-round, drive-everywhere, do-everything type of life. You stress about what you don't have and what you do have, and you think you or your kids are missing something in life, which is exactly the experience that society has set up for you.

So much of the news, media, and entertainment is designed to tell you your life isn't perfect. You often live outside your values by wanting what everyone else emphasizes is important, therefore trying to live your life around an illusionary "perfect life" on how society says you "should" live.

You rarely stop to question the status quo. Monday-morning blues, over-the-hump Wednesdays, thank-God-it's Fridays, and weekends. This is what it is like to remain on autopilot and virtually "asleep."

What might it be like to actually wake up from this redundant, predictable, Groundhog Day approach to life, family, and relationships?

wake up

This is your journey of awakening. It's for you to decide how the ride goes; how awake or asleep you would like your life to be; for you to choose your various options along the course and give them meaning.

It is important to remember that at every moment, there is a new opportunity to awaken. At every moment is another choice.

Unfortunately, during our ride, many of us don't pay attention to what is really going on. From birth, we have been conditioned through family and culture to blindly follow the "herd" and make that our standard of living, with little awareness or introspection. We have been trained to go on autopilot, so often being blind to our actions, without accessing a higher awareness.

So the question is, do you want to break the cultural conditioning and carve your own path for authentic living?

Since you are unique, what are the novel experiences you would like to experience with your family?

What are the one or two inspiring daily routines you would love to have in your life?

the waking parent

We are dancing between old and new paradigms of living. More people are recognizing that some of the rules and values that we are surrounded by in our culture don't align with the highest version of who we can be, nor with what we envision for our children. We sense this sort of melancholy, sadness, or even despair about the future for the next generations and what will come of our world and, simultaneously, see outrageous potential.

This waking up to what's not working has allowed many people to begin the process toward reevaluating their priorities and true values, leading to a deeper sense of wholeness. There is a tremendous surge for us parents to assist our children with tapping into their true nature and potential, and therefore, we awaken to this magic as well.

What is being observed in the waking transition is the focus of allowing ourselves and our children to authentically feel and express emotions, needs, talents, and uniqueness, rather than trying to fit into a cultural model of what reality "should" look like.

As this awareness comes more into reality for parents, more re-sources become available to assist us in this awakening movement. This places parenting at the forefront to influence future generations and rewire the cultural landscape.

Living with children provides everyone in the family with an op-portunity to grow. Holding this perspective is difficult to do in mo-ments when tempers flare. It is in those moments though, when you've just spent two hours trying to control your kids' behavior and ex-hausted your inner energy, that you realize that you've disconnected from your highest self. Once you have seen this "slip," you then have the opportunity to correct the course, reconnect, and proceed with love. It's in the course correction that the growth occurs. You get to rewire your system for love.

When is the last time you contemplated parenting as a way for both parent and child to learn to tap into their unlimited potential?

Where is your child most energized and inspired right now and how can you support them?

inner observer

To begin awakening, we must become an observer of our actions and reactions, thoughts and feelings. Like placing a magnifying glass over an object, beginning to observe oneself means seeing with greater clarity what is really going on. We awaken to our habits of how quickly we react with fear or frustration, anger or judgment. Observing requires a "pause" to help us process the patterns of our normal reactions.

Within our day-to-day reactions, it is often not "us" that is reacting but often stems from influences and experiences of the past. This pause in our awareness creates the opportunity to see the various new responses that are available for us and to choose how we interact with our child and the world around us.

To discover is to uncover, and while uncovering who you are not, and who or what is really influencing your decisions, the side effect is becoming more awake.

You then transfer this more wakeful presence to your children, imposing less of your beliefs and hardwired rules, and keeping a more expanded curiosity and playfulness in your relationships, so your kids can shape and map their reality of the world.

The daily situations that are most stressful are often the areas that require more observation and "pause."

What are your most stressful points throughout the day?
Pick a very specific moment and watch to see
how you "did" stress in that moment. What were you focused on?
How did you hold your body? How did you speak?
Be present and breathe with that moment
so that you can learn and release.

the aha moments

The pausing and the observing effortlessly create the aha moments. As the magnifying lens get closer and closer, you see things clearer and clearer. These moments of clarity are fun because we instantly see how we were missing things in our awareness while we were going about our daily business.

Imagine your child decides they no longer want to get dressed in the morning and you have to wrestle with them to get their clothes on. Then after the week of torture and bantering back and forth, you create this moment of pause where you realize that maybe something is not working, so you get clearer or magnify your awareness. You pause. You take a breath. You draw yourself into a new reality of what's really in front of you.

By creating a pause of clarity, you change your approach to being playful and tickling them, which gets them laughing and changes their focus. It takes the charge off both of you and places each of you in a state of ease.

The aha is in recognizing that for a week you have been reacting, been unfocused, unclear, and not present. The aha is the moment you reveal to yourself how non-resourceful you have been. You have been agitated and hung up on the problem, as opposed to focusing on a more connected solution.

It's a heightened level of awareness. One that is lighter, more energized, and more fun.

*What does it feel like when you realize
you have just experienced an aha moment?*

How grateful are you for the wake-up?

a unique cycle of life

Parenting is not a job, nor is it something to be "right" at. Parenting is a cycle of life, where you unfold and heal and simultaneously mentor little beings. You are guiding each other so you have the freedom to express yourselves fully, bring your gifts to the world in your unique style, with love. Agendas are dropped and expectations are released. The only job is to love each other no matter what.

For the parent, this means to be present, listen, focus, spend time with, and meet the child's needs of love and affection, while providing them room to grow as their rhythms demand. Watch them. They will show you the rhythms of their needs.

Sometimes they will want to be close, then want space, then want to hug, then to run, then need you, then not. It is up to you to follow their lead. As a parent you become a mentor to your child, and hopefully one who lives an inspired and authentic life.

Many parents today have difficulty adhering to the "I am the parent, do as I say" culture. It just doesn't feel right, especially as your consciousness expands. An awakened parent is one who honors a child's unique style while holding the space for where they are at in the moment. As a mentor, you set the stage by living an aware, conscious life—becoming an example of what is possible.

It is a practice of self-mastery to be able to show up in a deeper and more profound way for your family. If you choose to be yourself, authentic, and live the life you really want, your children will feel that. Your way of being becomes their way of living.

The next time you accuse your kids of doing something wrong,
pause and take a look in the mirror and see how
that resembles your own thoughts, feelings, or actions.
What could you do differently next time?
In small shifts like this, we begin to embody
a new way of seeing and moving in the world.

parenting as
your own awakening

Parenting is another of life's opportunities to become vastly more aware of who you really are. It quickly transforms your identity, your boundaries, your sense of who you think you are, and your perceptions of what the world is all about.

Parenting causes a metamorphosis, crumbling some of your old hardwired identities that have been developed early on while simultaneously creating a new version of you.

You must begin to surrender to the new life and now learn to work within the dynamics of an evolved family matrix. When you attempt to cling to the same person you were before having a child, there is often tremendous suffering. Remember when you needed to only consider yourself or partner when going out for an evening? Remember when you could get into your car in one minute? Remember when running to the store could happen on a whim? Remember life's spontaneity?

Surrender to the present or cling to the past.

How can you graciously let parts of you fall away
while simultaneously allowing for a new identity to emerge?

What is one part of your past that you must let go of
in order to bring more joy to your life now?

your little teachers

hildren have an amazing way of reorganizing what and how we prioritize our lives. Let's face it, children have the ability to call us on our bullshit. They point out the incongruence in how we speak, think, act, and feel.

They say, "Hey, you, wake up!" They point out that last week you told them one thing and this week you told them the opposite.

They draw out emotions in us, like anger and rage, that we may not normally express. They show us how simple life can be; how to find the joy in the little things. They show us how freedom really looks. They show us how to be present and in the moment. They show us focus, determination, and perseverance—and that nothing is impossible.

They are resilient, and have patience, flexibility, and resolve. They show you how to not take things personally; how to just move on, without a grudge. These little blessings remind us daily to cultivate the qualities and attitudes all the self-help books, gurus, and spiritual teachings have taught us for centuries and encourage us to discover within ourselves. The bookshelves of written material to help you with transformation and awakening are all summed up right in front of you.

If you choose to be present and aware, be mindfully with and consciously observe your children; they can teach you so much. If you're receptive to it, tuning in instead of tuning out, the gifts are limitless.

Can you find three key lessons that keep coming up with your kids, that they are attempting to help you learn or grow into? Are you needing to find more patience? Tolerance? Presence? Tenacity? What clues have you been given?

How can you begin to develop that trait within yourself to continue to grow and evolve?

expanding awareness

Surviving and thriving in this twenty-first century are two very different ways to live life. Existing is not living. There is life beyond surviving.

Surviving is about trying to be safe, secure, conservative, not taking chances, not growing, and just getting by.

Thriving, on the other hand, is about experiencing, expressing, and opening up to new options and possibilities for living.

The more you surrender to the flow of life with an inspired and clear mind, the more vitality for life you experi- **Existing is not living.** ence. The more you begin to surrender to and accept your current reality, the more clarity, poise, presence, and love you experience.

This is thriving as a human being and as a family unit in today's world.

*What would be the benefits to you and your children
if you focused on thriving in your own authentic style?*

*Can you take a moment and connect to your heart
and your inspired purpose?*

conscious living

Conscious living is not about denying what you are feeling, or repressing emotions, but it involves bringing awareness to what you are experiencing throughout the day.

Conscious living is like an on-off switch for most. You thrive and are present and aware one minute, then surviving and reactive and reflexive the next.

The key to this perspective is to be compassionately aware of exactly what you are feeling and how you are behaving whenever your awareness shows up. You can't force this.

The more attention and focus you place on "being aware," the more you become aware. Cultivating a heightened sense of awareness takes a different focus in your time and energy, and is worth the investment.

In time, you learn to trust and go with your own unique flow.

Love and joy can become your baseline.

Fear, frustration, or anger are there to remind you of a more primitive, less aware, and reactive version of you.

This is the dance of bouncing between an awakened and aware state versus an impulsive and auto-responsive sleep state.

Although aspects of life can be horribly painful, conscious living is about surrendering and loving the experience of being in the chaos; in the experience; in the present moment, where you are able to see the perfection and order that surrounds your life. Bringing that style of awareness and acceptance into your daily actions creates and nurtures a life with more meaning and depth. You get to observe the unique gifts of each individual interaction with others and live the experience from the perspective that everything is a divine gift or blessing.

Your daily experiences can now reflect this new, conscious reality. Time spent with your children and family will be more endearing as it reflects this awakened consciousness. You experience your kids as they are, being aware of your connectivity to them, how you share unique gifts, talents, and abilities, and how you continue to support and challenge one another for growth and conscious awareness.

In what ways are you helping to grow your conscious awareness?

How are you practicing this art of awareness so it becomes you?

3

practice

Parenting in the Moment, Day by Day

sur·ren·der

to cease resistance to; give in; give up oneself

I have provided for you a mantra at the end of each section to Find Magic in the Mess. Enjoy the playfulness, flow, and truth in each of the affirmations.

A new day, a new dawn. Some days will feel brutal, and others will feel brilliant. Fortunately, each day gives us an opportunity as parents to be awakened to ourselves and those for whom we care.

Although we may succumb at times to the sticky and muddy parts of life, we still have the opportunity to shoot for the moon within our awareness.

Since every interaction bears its own gifts, surrendering to the everydayness of parenting allows us to stay in the flow, observe what's in front of us, and maximize the love we share with one another. As we move into a lighter and more expansive awareness, we will feel or experience with fuller depth the areas we still tend to want to resist and control. The areas of resistance are the ones that are calling for greater surrender.

This chapter provides us as parents, and also as people, the opportunity to widen and broaden our perspective in everyday life, with supportive questions to further navigate our journey. This chapter is about how to turn everyday "stuff" into opportunities for greater growth and contribution.

Surrender to the everydayness.

gratitude over "manners"

Children learn how to operate in the world by mirroring you. Acquiring manners is no different. Apart from that, since children are authentic and genuine, a thank-you comes naturally when they are truly grateful.

Do you say thank you all the time? We all forget to say thank you even though we were told countless times to always have manners. When you are genuinely grateful though, you do remember. Regardless of the countless years of training to be the robot your parents thought you should be, you still say it when the feeling is there. And when the feeling is not there, you fake it. When you truly aren't grateful, you lie just because you were trained to be a robot. The thank-you becomes mindless and meaningless.

Do you want to teach your children to be robots? That's what you are doing when you tell them to say thank you when they are not grateful. Do you want to teach them to lie to others just to make others feel good? Is this an effective long-term strategy? You don't want to raise a liar, but you tell them to lie. Oh, it's just a little white lie. Or it's not "really" a lie. A lie is saying something that isn't true. If you tell your kids to say thank you when they don't mean it, it's a lie . . . right?

An example of how we do this as parents would be when someone brings the child something when they haven't asked for it, but the giver begs them for a thank-you. "What do you say? I brought you something." The child might be busy checking it out, feeling it, looking at it intently with curiosity, or perhaps really excited and still processing the surprise gift. They are just looking at it and enjoying the moment. The child didn't ask for it but is being begged to give praise immediately, for the instant gratification of the adult.

If you say thank you when you sincerely mean it, your kids learn to say thank you as well, because they feel your energy when you're genuinely grateful. And when they feel the same genuine gratitude, they too will know the appropriate response that comes with that. They associate genuine gratitude with a feeling, energy, and emotion; they are not thinking about pleasing your ego.

Being grateful does not come from a thought. It comes from a feeling. From your heart. So don't worry about what they say, but instead watch how the thank-you is expressed naturally in their own authentic way.

Stop taking it personally if your child forgot to say thank you. I have seen many parents and grandparents getting not only angry but also disappointed and guilt-tripping children for poor manners. If the kids feel it, truly feel it, they will reply, in their own style and manner, when appropriate. Again, you can't control it. What we would want to see and hear is a genuine appreciation either verbally or shown in their actions.

I went to a health-food store with my daughter where I bought her a fruit smoothie she wanted. She didn't say thank you for the purchase. My unconscious conditioning could have made sure she did. I could have said, "Hey, you forgot to say something!" That's not what I did, because in reality I didn't buy it for her so that I could hear a thank-you. Interestingly, when we pulled in the driveway, she sat up, leaned forward, kissed my cheek, and left the car. That was her thank-you, in her time and way, totally authentic.

Forcing a child to say thank you seems to say that you are showing a person respect. This old belief is based on fear of how we will look in the eyes of others. This is your issue. Not your child's problem. Don't make it their issue. They are not bad for being truthful, nor disrespectful by being authentic. They are not at fault for being themselves.

If you find yourself saying, "What do you say?" or "Say thank you . . . ," then reflect on your own behaviors and begin to be grateful for what you have by saying thank you. The parent who is authentically grateful and expresses it regularly bears offspring who follow suit. If need be, teach yourself to look for blessings and gifts in your own day-to-day life and say thank you in your own style first, before putting pressure on your kids to repeat a meaningless response. Be congruent in your actions and surely your children will mirror them. If they don't, ask questions without judging them or their response.

Is a smile not enough? Is a squeal of excitement not enough? Are arms raised in elation not enough? Is jumping up and down not enough? No. The mind, the ego, says no. The mind says the child must say these specific words. They must say thank you. It's like saying, "Here is your script, now read your lines." For heaven's sake, is emotional expression not enough?

I have seen children jumping for joy, clearly elated, only to be deflated by an emotionless parent instructing them to say thank you. I could feel the energy instantly shift as their natural expression and state of joy is stifled, as the child is forced to stoop to obeying rigid societal rules. They have given the ultimate prize to their proud parent by saying thank you. This parent could have taken the initiative and proclaimed, "Wow, your jumping sure shows you are loving that! . . . My pleasure!"

Kids may not say thank you, but they have authentic ways of showing genuine gratitude. A hug. A kiss. A coy smile. A big smile. Wiggly fingers and toes. Kicking legs. Jumping. Spinning. Running. Laughing. Screaming. And I am pretty sure you have seen adults express themselves the same ways. You, when truly grateful, show your emotions far beyond what words can convey. Words can be so boring and mundane. Enjoy keeping a keen eye on your child for their expression of gratitude, and you'll find yourself delighted by the experience. It keeps you present and curious. Focusing on gratitude expressions allows you to stay present and learn more about your child's authentic style of self-expression.

Can you accept that a thank-you can come in different forms?
How does your child naturally express gratitude?

Gratitude is an expression, not a thought.

letting go of "thank you"

Consider this: When we are taking care of someone who is ill, we require no thank-you. This is because we are selflessly serving with our heart and spirit. And no words are needed. Just serving someone who is ill is a gift unto itself.

Mahatma Gandhi said, "Service which is rendered without joy helps neither the servant nor the served. But all other pleasures and possessions pale into nothingness before service which is rendered in a spirit of joy."

So from that, if you bring someone toast for breakfast, why would a thank-you be required? Are you serving them selflessly, or are you serving them to be validated for the good deed you did? It is only the ego that needs to hear thank you, because the ego abides by rules, and our culture dictates that rules have to look a certain way.

Your soul serves just to serve, without a need to be reimbursed. Chances are, your definition of how your family shows love and appreciation has been shaped by what society dictates is "right." What I am asking here is that you go beyond your usual story, so we as parents can experience an expansive, more authentic range of emotional expression.

Your ego does things to get love or feel significant, and it requires acknowledgment. If you are getting your emotions stirred by not hearing what you expect to hear, it is your preprogrammed ego getting offended and not feeling loved, significant, or validated. Your ego wants a return on its investment, or it feels slighted. Children don't think in these terms, adults do.

I know you would agree that having your ego stroked is not what parenting is about. It's not about you; it's not to get love or feel significant. It's to give love. And giving love and serving for the sake of the soul requires no return. Because serving and giving love is the return. It is more than enough, and more than a verbal thank-you could ever provide. Your growing child is the one who needs to feel the love and who needs to feel significant. You are beyond that. You are an adult.

When serving your children their breakfast,
can you find it within yourself to be grateful to be able to serve them,
and let go of waiting for the thank-you?

Can you accept the part of you that seeks love, approval,
and significance? Ask yourself how you feel
when your service is not validated by others.

Selfless service is of the soul.

the myth of forgiveness

Could forgiveness be a great hoax? What does it mean to forgive? What does it imply when you say it? Why is it so damn difficult? And when we think we have forgiven, have we really?

Most of us think that we must forgive to move on; that something bad happened to us at one point in our life, involving a parent, sibling, teacher, or friend, and in order to heal the wounds of the past, we must forgive. Forgiveness comes from a place of judgment.

We feel it is our way to freedom and peace.

There is a more efficient and effortless way. In fact, people spend years trying to forgive to no avail. Trying to forgive a person or make peace with an incident in which one feels wronged takes forever, if it happens at all.

How many times have you told your child to say sorry, only to have the other party respond with the status quo response "I forgive you," or "It's okay"?

Both parties couldn't be more insincere, and we know it. As parents, we think we are teaching our children about respect. But what this teaches them is the need to say what others think we should say and lie if it goes against our gut instinct because this is the way the world works and this is the way we gain acceptance. What a questionable strategy. We are teaching our children to be disconnected from their true feelings. Imagine as an adult, you get irritated waiting too long for a meeting at your lawyer's office. You snap on the defenseless receptionist. The lawyer storms out and tells you to apologize to his employee. You say, "I'm sorry," and he of course instructs her to say, "I forgive you," and harmony is restored, right? This strategy does not fly when we are adults, nor does it fly as kids. It's going through the motions, but the sentiment expressed is untrue.

If our child has done their best in that moment, what should they be sorry for?

If we as parents have done our best in the moment, what should we be sorry for?

"I forgive" in our culture means "I know you did something wrong to me, and I now am okay with the fact that you wronged me and made a bad decision." This idea encourages a victim mentality. There is no release from this approach, and that's why years later, people are still in therapy talking about the same event. Forgiving others implies that you are still a victim of wrongdoing.

All this shows is that you have not accepted that you were given the experiences that you experienced. "I forgive" says that you have yet to find the gift that is there for you from the experience. The same goes with your child. They are meant and designed to experience all that they experience. Experiences that activate elation, joy, inspiration, and pleasure, as well as anger, sadness, sorrow, or pain. They wouldn't have experienced it if it did not serve them in any way.

You as well as your children will have a broad range of experiences that are all necessary to experience, not just the ones that feel good.

So if we go back to the simple truth that each experience is designed to be experienced, then no one needs to apologize, and no one needs to forgive.

You and your children don't need to forgive yourself, anyone, or anything for events that have happened to you in your life, to achieve healing and peace. It's a fallacy and one of our grand illusions. This is not to say there are not consequences to choices, but the consequences are a necessary part of the human experience. To achieve peace from these necessary experiences, one first needs to be able to see value in the experience. Although not an easy task, the pathway to peace comes in resolution, not in a concept of forgiveness. Resolution into peace comes in the way of showing our kids exactly how the action that was done to them serves them in some way—and often, upon introspection, in many ways. If one doesn't train the mind to see the value, resentment is the only possible outcome. You have to dig, and dig deep, for the value to your life. Find enough value, resentment clears to become gratitude, acceptance, and a true full body-mind resolution.

Every action will have a reaction. As you begin to awaken, it becomes more and more effortless to see how every circumstance is perfect, how there are equal amounts of pain and pleasure that are created from a situation. Take a look around. It is in times of our deepest despair that we connect into what is real. This is transformation. Stop protecting yourself and your kids from life; see, feel, and embrace the value in every experience.

Imagine the freedom experienced through surrender and acceptance. Imagine how you would live and grow if you accepted and were grateful that every event is required exactly as it appears solely to add value to your life journey. Every event is a gift, and when you acknowledge and accept the gift, when you open the package and celebrate it, you won't want to change a thing. Teach this to your kids. Teach them the value of finding and discovering the gift in the wounds; the gifts in the arguments, in the insults, in betrayals, even in the teasing and in the bullying to certain extents.

"What's the benefit to you for being teased?" *Well, I was sad and cried in front of my teacher.* "And the benefit in that?" *She felt bad for me.* "And the benefit in that?" *She got mad and told the principal.* "And the benefit in that?" *He suspended the kid.* "And the benefit in that?" *He went home.* "How did that benefit anyone?" *He stopped teasing others.* "So by being teased, and sharing your emotions, you helped to stop him from teasing other kids?" *Yes, I guess.* "So by being teased you also got to be the hero to many other kids?" *Hmmm, I guess so. (Child lightens up . . .)* Life continues to give us gifts, packaged in ways we could have or would have never imagined or anticipated. This is the art of surrendering and accepting. This is the skill set leading to gratitude.

Your children will interact with other children to develop character traits. Some friends will bring out courage. Some will bring out peace. Some will bring about focus, and some will bring out empathy. All the family members and friends intertwine to bring wholeness to the individual. We all contribute to one another's wholeness. There is nothing to forgive and everything to embrace.

Pick one challenge you are currently having within your own life.
Can you come up with ten to fifteen benefits
to you of this occurring right now?

Can you widen your perspective to see the gift
in all the challenges life throws your way?

I accept life for the gifts it brings me.

sharing

Why do we place such a high value on having our kids share? Why are you trying to make them share? Are you scared they won't be liked? Are you worried that they will not learn the value in working as a team?

What if you let them hoard everything? What would happen? Would they never share another thing for the rest of their life?

What's the worry? Pause to feel the worry, breathe into the discomfort, and open up to new understanding.

Your child will learn how to participate in life and with others. If they want to be part of a community of kids, they will learn how to operate within that. Sometimes it will be the easy way, sometimes the painful way.

If you would like your kids to share, and see value in that, it's helpful for you as the parent to be able to hold a double perspective. By this I mean that sharing is a skill that is inherent to survival of the tribe. It's something that is and has been ingrained for thousands of years.

For most of human existence, if you didn't share food or resources within the tribe, many people would die. So it's something to be acknowledged and understood as an essential ingredient for human survival. At the same time, *not sharing* was equally as important. If other tribes came along and you shared everything with them, and gave it all away, you and your kin would be in trouble. At this point, it's extremely important to be stingy. You don't want to share. In fact, if you look around you, even in your neighborhood, a plethora of examples exist of not sharing. Consider most yards, driveways, cars, homes, and so on. They are all unshared, and if someone just came by and said, "I'm going to have a barbecue in your yard," you might have something to say about it. If someone came and asked you for your car keys, you might get a little guarded. If someone came and said, "Can I relax on your couch?" I think you can see you might be slightly challenged, because you have decided these are yours. Sharing isn't always the most advantageous thing to do. And for this same reason, your child sometimes draws a similar boundary to what is his or hers.

So sharing and stingy are opposite poles of the spectrum of give-and-take, and we tend to idealize a particular trait because it's seen as "nice" instead of appreciating and understanding its value. Sometimes just being able to hold this double perspective is more than enough to abide your intolerance, frustration, or irritation surrounding the idea of sharing. Both sharing and being stingy are valuable human traits, in different circumstances.

Allow me to ask you a few questions about sharing. Do you share your dreams, your genuine feelings, your loves, your deepest desires, your most intimate thoughts, your challenges, and your emotions? Do you share your body with your partner regularly? Do you share kisses, hugs, and affection regularly? Do you hide any of these, tuck them away just for you to know, or are you open to sharing with others your full authentic self? I'm talking about your dreams, desires, and most intimate experiences. Do you keep them to yourself because you are scared of looking foolish, or being disappointed or let down? Do you hold back compliments to others, or remain reserved by withholding your expressions of sadness or happiness? What do you conceal, hold back, contain, or "not share" about yourself?

The point is, instead of concerning yourself with your child sharing these superficial things, allow yourself to look within and to take the next step to discover more about you and your willingness to share.

You were taught as a child not to be selfish and not to hoard things, but did that really work for you? You hold on to guilt, anger, hurt feelings, trauma, and your talents. You also hold on to compliments, visions, courage, and love. Look beyond the material world with what you practice and teach.

Can you make a list of all the areas where others are not benefiting from you sharing your body, emotions, ideas, intellect, or natural gifts?

What action can you take immediately to share yourself more to others so they benefit from you being alive?

**Giving and receiving
are both valuable and important.**

let them work it out

've often wondered why parents drive themselves mad trying to keep the peace between kids. Children have to learn how to create peace through anger, conflict, and resolution. When you interrupt, they can't move through their own growth.

Ask yourself why you are holding on to the idea that there should be only peace in the moment. Let them rumble and work it out! After all is said and done, if someone isn't there to save the day, they come to an agreement or one is victorious and the other is defeated. Both are learning experiences. It is all an experience, and sometimes kids have their feelings hurt and sometimes they don't. You can't save them.

A useful approach could be first asking yourself if this is a dangerous situation. Are any of the kids actually at risk of serious injury? Without kids being at risk for physical injury, the next thing to consider is if this is just you trying to be controlling or not liking violence or conflict. Beyond serious injury, most of the tension felt within you is the distaste for conflict. Most kids can end up sloughing it off. And if they don't, you then have but another opportunity for them to find value in the experience.

Potentially, overpossessiveness of keeping the peace prevents children from gaining the gifts of having a rival—a situation and relationship that can challenge them to grow.

What if you looked at the crying child or the one who "lost" as having gained a learning experience? What are they learning in that moment?

I allow my child to feel strong and weak.

peaceful waiting

We've all done it. Ripped the unsightly scab off early because we just wanted it gone. And what happens every time we take a scab off before the time is right? More pain, more sensitivity, more bloodshed, and longer healing time. Inevitably we find ourselves having to wait for the body to form another scab because of our impatience to be rid of it. Maybe it's ugly, maybe it's itchy, and maybe it's annoying. Who cares, we just want it gone.

Beneath the scab, tremendous healing is taking place. Cellular repair, cleanup, immune responses, and new cell formation is happening every second. It seems like the scab is so static, but yet, underneath, a vital and complex process of healing is occurring. The key: When the healing is done, the scab falls off.

As humans we might call this "letting go." You can't force the healing; it just happens. You can't force the change; it just happens.

You can't force the letting go; it just happens. If you remove the scab early, more pain and prolonged healing are the results. This is the same for everything else in life.

Remember, we teach our kids to not pick off the scab, because when it is ready, it will fall off. And intellectually, we know this. We just fail to see how this little example could apply to so many areas of our children's development as well as our interaction with them. Here is the irony in our day-to-day.

Forcing the scab off is like trying to make your kids walk before they crawl, read before they are ready, or resolve an argument without listening.

There is a magnificent timing to all that is going on in our lives.

Where are you trying to force things to happen instead of letting it flow? Where, in fact, do you require more patience, time, and healing? Maybe more patience with your goals and aspirations, more time for that fulfilling relationship you've been wanting, or more healing for that health situation to improve. There is a timing and rhythm to life, and the people you meet and the places you go each day can all be part of the process. You won't always be able to see life's underlying organization working for you. Trust is required, just like waiting for the scab to heal. Know that within and around you, there is an organizing field of intelligence that is working for you, not against you.

Your children have their own rhythms of life. Patience.

What is one area of life in which you need more patience to allow the perfect timing to unfold?

What is one step you can take today to feel more empowered and connected to its unfolding?

_____

There is a perfect timing and rhythm to our lives.

it is what it is, until it isn't

So we had a bad day, week, or even month. It happens, and it's far from fun. It's okay to wallow for a little as we regroup and restore our energy. Can certain things slow us down from achieving a more resilient state?

It's so easy at times to cling, to wrap ourselves in the past, even if it's moments ago. For many, we battle the demon of attaching ourselves to what has occurred, perhaps mishaps with our kids, misfortunes, things we said, fights we had, ways we acted and reacted and lashed out . . .

It's so easy to do this. We become hardwired into guilt, shame, sadness, and blame.

These concepts keep us stuck in a false and distorted reality, one that keeps us from releasing and feeling free, because our entire body-mind is still chained to the past. Still reacting, still stressing, still defending, still replaying the same event or incident over and over again, like a record player stuck on the same song.

This mental game of remaining anchored in the past is far from pleasant. There is no peace, growth, ease, serenity, sanity, or freedom.

Staying stuck robs us of who we are and keeps us emotionally blinded to all of life's gifts and blessings. How do we break this destructive cycle?

The road to release and freedom is surrender and acceptance. It's that simple.

If you and your kids were not meant to experience something, why would you experience it? If you missed out on an opportunity, why do you think you were supposed to "miss out"? So much of our distress comes from the idea that something wasn't supposed to happen, or that we missed out on an opportunity. It's not easy, but the connected parent must discover the blessing in the setback, the gift in the wound, and the joy in the distress. We ask that of our kids and must practice the same ourselves.

I worked with a woman in her thirties whose mother had left her father when she was six. Her mother moved the entire family in the summer, telling the kids they were going to visit family. When they got there, she then told them that she was splitting up with their dad and that they were not returning home. Instantly, this girl lost her dad and that entire side of her family. As we went through a healing process and began to balance out her perceptions of the experience, she began to see, one by one, how what she thought was lost and was gone forever was actually still in her life, just in a different way. By the end of the process, she was in tears, calling her mom and thanking her for doing what she had done, because if not, this woman would not be who she is today. She realized, through the process, that for her evolution as a human being, she had to experience what she did, as hard and difficult as it was at the time.

As challenging as it sometimes may seem, there is a way through. What you experience as a family always holds an opportunity. A death, a job loss, a separation, a sickness, anything and everything we face, no matter how hard to comprehend, presents a unique experience for you as a parent, and for your family, if you choose to find it. This is true in the day-to-day as well. A rough day and short temper that got the best of you—these setbacks shape us and prepare us for the future.

Conversely, what you don't experience as a family, you were not meant to experience together. If you "miss out" on an experience, just remember, try to resist the pull of envy and regret. Instead, simply accept that the experience is not necessary for your journey at this point in time. Understand that all experiences are not necessary for your family's journey together. The Joneses' experience does not need to be your experience.

Simply stated, if you experienced it, it was necessary. Use it to grow. If you didn't experience it, it wasn't necessary yet or perhaps never will be. It is futile to stress about the past or future. Practice surrender and acceptance while seeing the value in an experience you've had or did not have; the timing of your experiences are always perfect.

What setback have you suffered as a parent, without seeing the benefit?
How can you use that experience to grow and do better going forward?

What areas of life are you constantly stressing about because it hasn't happened yet?

Life is bringing exactly what we need.

forget serious

As parents, when we are fully present, there is only room for love, joy, and laughter. If you are not laughing often, you are too serious. Seriousness is rigidity, and rigidity lends itself to disease and sickness, both mentally and physically. For you, your family's sake, and everyone's well-being, you may want to loosen your own reins.

The more present you are with your kids—watching their facial expressions, their dancing, their clumsiness, their playfulness; listening to them talk—the more laughter and joy you realize they bring. Laughter is healing.

It's only when you have an agenda that you get really serious. How many times have you said, "Seriously, we need to get going"; "Seriously, we need to eat now"; "Seriously, finish cleaning"; "Seriously, your game starts in one hour, let's go"? Seriously, seriously, seriously.

Laughter is healing.

When our kids don't want to follow our agenda, we may try to coerce them with phrases like "all kidding aside," or "get serious for a minute," or "get real." If we can't convince them to get serious like us, then we get angry. If that doesn't make them spring into action, our next move is to guilt them into obeying us by saying, "If you don't do this, that will happen." This is how we try to remain in control of them.

So often parents create an environment that goes from laughter to anger to guilt, all so our kids conform to our agenda. Where else might we do this? And with whom? We teach them to replace laughter, joy, happiness, and love with seriousness, anger, fear, and guilt. That's a nasty trade-off, isn't it?

Count how many times you say "seriously," or use a serious tone, and I will tell you how many times you've created unnecessary stress in your body. Count how many times you focus on where you "need to go," and I will tell you how often you aren't present in joy and laughter. Remember, what you feel, your children feel. You are one. They're little sponges, absorbing everything in their environment—including your every move, what you say, and what you don't say.

What are the rules around the house that seem to force you to get serious?

Who set those rules for you?

I find joy within and around me.

what's the rush?

Why are you rushing? Do you have a hard-core schedule you are trying to follow? If so, why? For whom? Why are you doing it? Is it enjoyable? Are your kids going to remember this schedule fondly? Is this in the best interest of the family? Is everyone better off? Does this produce greater well-being for the family unit? Does a crazy schedule meet the authentic needs of your kids?

The job of parenting is to create an environment rich in learning, exploring, and expressing—a home and lifestyle that supports and challenges for optimal growth.

Children tend to experience and remember the emotion of life, more so than the content. If the prevailing mood in your home is hectic, frantic, and time-obsessed, that may overshadow the true pleasure that could be enjoyed from any particular activity. Most parents desire a relaxed and productive flow to life. Most kids perform better under those circumstances as well.

Are you too overextended in your schedule and, therefore, too disconnected as a family?

What is something in your schedule that does not represent your highest values that can be eliminated to free up more downtime?

I balance my pace of life.

laughter

How many people come out of a comedy show looking stressed? We know that laughter heals and feels so good. Your wacky, zany, crazy kids will help you to heal your serious wounds if you can chill out long enough to allow it to happen.

Laughter extends and opens up the structure of your body and allows energy to flow freely, liberating compression or contraction into flow and ease. Laughter facilitates greater communication between the spiritual energy and your body. Extension and openness will facilitate health and healing, and activate life energy for healing of disease. Laughter creates what spiritual teachers, chiropractors, yogis, and energy healers look to create for mankind: freedom, flexibility, strength, energy, healing, and sanity!

Try laughing and keeping your neck and spine and body rigid. You can't do it.

Staying present combined with laughter is a recipe for well-being. Laughter nurtures a family to be lighter and more loving.

Kids yelling at each other? Laugh. Getting frustrated at no one listening? Laugh. There aren't too many things better than a great belly laugh. Think about it. It's therapeutic and costs nothing. It can be done anywhere, anytime. It changes your entire biochemistry and trips hormones of joy. It's orgasmic! Be often in laughter. Surround yourself in laughter. Laugh as much as possible with your kids; watch them in presence and joy, as they are the greatest comedians on the planet. And most important, laugh at yourself.

What can you do to honor the more free-spirited, flexible parts of yourself?

Laughter is a gateway to my essence.

picky eaters

et's explore if you have any picky bones in your body. You aren't particular about the clothes you wear, the way your hair looks, the partner you chose, or the house you live in. You are not picky about the decor in your home, your friends, or the occupation you chose. You just take everything as it comes in stride and have no preference for anything in life. Is this correct?

Let's establish that you, in fact, are picky. Admit it.

Being picky, selective, or particular when it comes to food is a mechanism of survival. It is how we can decipher nutritious versus poisonous. What if your child has a sensitivity to a food that you don't? What if you keep putting something in front of them that feels wrong to their taste buds? What if they know this, and they are in tune with the needs of their body? What if it's not the right time for them to eat? What if their needs are different from yours? All this is possible, isn't it?

You can almost bet they are more in tune with their needs in the moment than you are. You may have lost this skill. You may have become unconscious and disconnected from your inner needs and rhythms.

You don't know what your kids will like. But the dinner table is a great place for them to explore choice. Your inability to cook is not the reason they are not choosing to eat that dish. They are not taking into account the hours you prepared in the kitchen like a world-class chef. They are not considering the sweat you endured to prepare the fine meal. All they know is whether they want to eat it. So please remember it is not a personal attack on your skills or the cuisine you create.

For the sake of learning, let's replace the word *picky* with *particular* and *selective*. Those are traits that you would see of value in your children's future. The fact that your children actually know what they like and don't like, and can vocalize this, is important to you. As a teen and adult, these would potentially mean their internal standards are high and they have healthy self-esteem.

The more you put an emotional charge into what they eat, the more they feel the response. The more you complain to your friends about their eating habits, the more issues you create.

Relax, they will not starve. You don't need to serve 1,001 things. You don't need to appease them but instead become familiar to their rhythms of eating. You also may want to evaluate what choices you are giving them. Kids don't need a ton of calories. Amazingly they will eat what they need. As long as you don't force them to ignore the mechanism in their body, they will finish when they have had enough. To force your kids to finish food is forcing them to bypass all internal signals indicating fullness for the approval of their parents or the rewards of dessert. It's important to allow kids to listen to their own bodies.

Laugh at yourself for getting so worked up at times about food and what your kids are eating. Keep the tradition of eating fun, light, social. Keep love, community, and family in the foreground of your awareness.

What habits and rules about food did you grow up with?
Are the rules outdated and needing some revisions, and if so,
what would you do differently?

———————————

**I know what I require
to nourish all parts of me.**

they will learn

We have trust as parents that in the first two years of life our children will learn how to walk and talk on their own, two of the most difficult tasks humans learn to master.

Learning to walk: from lying, to rolling, to pushing up, to sitting, to crawling, to standing, to walking—some of the most complex tasks for mankind. There are so many processes happening within the body-mind system for this to happen, it's incomprehensible to any rational mind. It is so big, it is beyond any of us to fully understand. But we trust this will happen. It's a natural part of evolution. We don't sit and show them. We don't crawl and show them. We don't walk to show them. They learn what they need to do in order to move around. And we trust that they will innately learn this, in their own time, without our having to "teach" them.

They learn to speak from nothing, from "goos," "gagas," and grunts to gibberish, to sort-of words, to words, to meaningful sentences. It is guided by forces beyond what we can imagine, and we trust this will happen naturally. All we do is speak, and they learn how to get there on their own. No teaching. They do it through keen observation, mimicking, sounding, practice, modeling, and more practice.

Assuming there are no major neurological interferences to their functioning, most children learn these tasks well. Two of the most complex tasks we could possibly imagine, done by the first few years of life, all through their natural development, in their own time, and without force. They are guided by their natural abilities through evolution and growth.

Then after these processes of development are complete, we tend to lose trust in the process.

We then decide that we have to control how our child learns and develops. Some appear to think that the child becomes instantly incapable of learning on their own. At this junction in the road, adults now know exactly what they must learn, at what age they must learn it, and because we know what's best for our children, the adults will teach these inadequate little ones. We construct rules; insist that they all of a sudden have to sit down to learn; that they have to spend six to eight hours a day learning. Like they haven't been learning every minute for the first five years of life. We now decide how this "learning" must happen and in what context. We then put pressure on them to learn in this most unnatural way. We begin to obsess about the timing of learning and attempt to control that. They just finished learning the most complex tasks all by themselves! Then we ignore their innate abilities in an attempt to impress upon them what we think they must learn, in the precise time we dictate, all so we can pass judgment on their success or failure.

The question is, where does the trust go? Why would we want to interfere with the child's development? They learn to walk and talk on their own, just by being around people. They figure it out in the perfect time for them. They don't start in a particular month like September, then end the learning process in June. They don't start learning on Monday and end on Friday. Learning takes place all day, every day of the week; they are learning in each moment what they are innately able to learn at that time. Nothing more, nothing less. Preparing children for life is one thing. Attempting to control, stress, determine, accelerate, and label the timing of the learning process is another.

Do some children take longer? Of course! Do some take less time? Of course! Children learn all tasks on their own unique schedule just as they do when learning to walk and talk. Do all kids have an inherent love of learning? Yes. Just watch them in the first few years of life—they are joyful and happy and love learning.

When we decide to place rules on their learning and create expectations that are to be met, we get serious again! They are constantly being judged. If our expectations are not met, kids are immediately labeled slow in that area. "They lack talent. They aren't a natural." If they took a few months longer to walk, would you label them not talented in walking? If they were slower by a few months to learn a language, would you say they were not talented at speaking? No, it just wasn't the right time yet. But we would trust they would learn it.

What if we just dropped our expectations and provided them with space, time, and resources and let them develop on their own time and in their own way? What if we made learning fun and free of expectation? So many parents stress over their child's not meeting expectations that are based on a highly structured learning process taking place from September to June, five days a week.

Celebrate the love of learning. Respect and appreciate the process, not the outcome. The waking parent knows that learning is a daily, lifelong process of discovery. We never, ever stop learning. Every novel experience we have is another learning opportunity within the process.

If provided the resources, kids will learn all they need to bring their gifts to the world and to follow their dreams and passions. Those who innately love math will use it. Those who don't won't.

Respect and appreciate the process, not the outcome.

Just as they needed to learn to walk and talk to survive, they will learn what is needed to develop their natural abilities and thrive. What does thriving mean anyway? Regardless of what you think they should learn, they will eventually learn what they want and will automatically gravitate toward activities that develop and strengthen their natural talents and abilities.

Don't worry, parents. Your children will be successful in their own way. They will eventually follow their dreams, whether you like it or not. The question is, how much are you going to pressure them with your priorities, only to delay this process? They will eventually follow their passions. You can't stop it, and why would you want to? You can only allow it, and so you might as well do so in such a way that they can express their talents and gifts to the world as early as possible. This will allow them to enjoy a long, passionate, and exciting life, in whatever capacity that means for them. Instead of resenting the constant exertion of rigid parental controls, they'll appreciate being given the latitude to explore and discover what thrills them.

Allowing them freedom from the shackles of having to learn everything in a particular sequence will nurture the spirit of your child and will enable them to explore as they need, in the time that is needed. Stay open, stay flexible, and stay in the rhythms of the day. Your child, like seasons, uses different resources of energy at different times. Be prepared and ready to embrace whatever they need, whenever they need it, and they will feel loved and nurtured in the learning process. Surrender less to schedules and time lines.

Different learning happens at different times. Sometimes children may need to build their physical strength over their intellectual. Sometimes they need to build their emotional energy, yell, and scream before they can think clearly. Ever felt like screaming, just to clear your head? There are different rhythms and cycles that happen throughout the day, that go beyond the rational mind, that cannot be explained by experts, charts, or graphs. We need to look deeper. We need to listen. Asking questions like "What are they needing right now?" will help you to stay mentally flexible and in tune with the rhythm they require.

Can you surrender to their pace of learning?
How can you support and acknowledge them along the way?

Learning is all day, every day, for life.

embrace inconvenience

The truth is that when you commit to having a child, you commit to a life of inconvenience. You left your previous life behind; a life of coming and going, doing what you want, showering when you want, eating when you want, meeting every egocentric desire you can possibly imagine, and indulging your every whim. You left that life. It is long gone, and it is the parent who clings or attempts to regain the freedom enjoyed in the old life who suffers. It's time to release the idea of rewinding time and instead move forward. That's your past; your children are your future. Their needs take precedence over yours.

Inconvenience is called sacrifice. Sacrifice is what you signed up for by becoming a parent. If you wanted to preserve your old life, your old ego needs, your old way of being, you shouldn't have had a child. But you had one, and so the sooner you recognize that you came together because you were ready to retire the old version of you, the sooner you will find freedom in this sacrifice. Moving into a place of service, growth, and contribution is a spiritual contract you made with your child. They didn't enter into this world saying they were going to be convenient, meet your every need, and follow your every command. Your new reality is quite the opposite.

They will test every facet of your ego, to get you to accept that inconvenience is part of being a parent. The harder you fight it, the harder the ego works to retain its previous identity and the harder parenting is. Worse still, the more you will disconnect from your child.

Breastfeeding, which is most often the parents' decision unless adoption or medical reasons require otherwise, is a perfect example of inconvenience. Watching my wife go through what she did to feed our children, I realized that in my eyes it was an act of pure love.

We saw and knew the compelling benefits of providing our children with the most profound nutrients available on the planet while simultaneously embracing the pains that come with it. Regardless of the pain, sleep deprivation, emotional stress, and frustration, the inconvenience of breastfeeding was not able to sway our compelling vision to serve our children with optimal physical and emotional nourishment.

Successful breastfeeding is a team effort, because there are so many conveniences that would allow and compel parents to throw in the towel. What were the options two hundred years ago? Either the child breastfeeds or the child dies.

Too many conveniences of modern times lend themselves to strong minds but weakened visions, and children suffer because convenience is placed ahead of what is optimal. The ego can quickly lose sight of what is most beneficial for the child, to have its own needs met. When you focus on the child, the rhythms of the child's needs are at the helm of the decision-making process. This is purely inconvenient. Your true essence has a knowing of what the next step is.

Holding an expanded vision can get tiring. Succumbing to the conveniences of everyday life is well . . . just that—convenient. And vision and convenience do not usually go hand in hand. When you are coming from convenience, you are focusing on your needs or what the culture is setting as a standard. You are not focusing on what you know in your heart to be true.

On the other hand, when you know what to do through holding a heartfelt vision, without having to rationalize, this is spirit. Once you say, "I know what is true in my heart," then you do whatever is inconvenient to get it done. Don't get me wrong, it is okay to have your needs met as parents but not at the expense and sacrifice of the well-being of your child. The child needs you. Your child needs you for safety, love, protection, and guidance. The ego makes decisions based on convenience rather than a spiritual knowing based on love and sacrifice.

Convenience is for the bachelor or bachelorette or the retired. Inconvenience is for the parent. Can you learn to love the variety and inconvenience that parenting has to offer? The greatest gift of being in a relationship is that of love, sacrifice, and inconvenience. Embrace it.

Where have you been indecisive about a situation with your child, and how can you connect to what is in the best interest of your child?

What is one thing with your child you know
you can hold to a higher standard?

I listen to my inner voice
and make decisions through that space.

lose control

So you think you have control? You're in control?

You think you have control over your kids' actions, reactions, yelling, fighting, and roughhousing? Forget about it. You don't stand a chance.

It's painful not to have control sometimes, isn't it? No matter how hard you try, no matter how much or often you make "the stern face," wave your finger, pull your hair, stomp your feet . . . your kids just don't care. What is even more frustrating is that you know in your heart that your nagging makes no difference and, in fact, goes against the natural flow of "you," the natural flow of spirit within you. Remember when you were a kid and deep down you tuned your parents out when they were going off on their tangents? Laughable.

Isn't it tiring to be someone you're not? It is so much work to try to control others, to attempt to control your environment, to try to make it happen, when it just won't. Trying is so hard. When will you give up the fight, the struggle, the frustration, and the anger? You know in your core that your kids don't respond in a healthy way to your manic ways.

Take a look in the mirror when you are really losing it. You look like an animal, a crazed animal—like a wild species that has been through a battle for survival. You sound like nails on a chalkboard, shrill if you will, with a lack of rationality.

So when is enough really enough?

How much longer will you continue this path of rants and disconnected reality? Your family is watching. They are listening. They are absorbing the very meaning and focus you give to events and circumstances. Those will become their meanings that they will use in their life. They watch how you respond and react to them. They watch how you move, breathe, and hold your energy when you are under stress.

It's time to tune inward. Calm down. Take a time-out, and put the brakes on.

As you put the brakes on, you become more present. In this present moment is your breath, your movement, and your focus. How you pay attention to the quality of these will influence not only your life but also the life of your child and everyone around you. How you master your breath, movement, and focus will demonstrate to them how you respond to the pressures of life. You will set the standard for the young, impressionable eyes.

So what meaning will you give to your day, to the yelling and fighting, the glass that was dropped and broke, the messy room, the stains that won't come out? What about when you are having a disagreement with your spouse or partner? Can you stay present with all this stuff? The things that weren't planned, that you don't enjoy, and that you are not in control of? How will you breathe through these situations? How adaptable are you? How will you move your body? Where will you place your focus? Your kids are watching; how do you want them to breathe, move, and sound when they are in your shoes?

You may not have control, but you have something much grander: your awareness.

Where can you use this awareness to your advantage, not only to retain some semblance of calm but to be of true service to yourself and your family?

Once you have the ability to accept that you have no control over others and their behavior, only then will you be free.

How can you surrender to the flow of the day,
without having to try to control the details?

Pick an area where you feel you need to be in control.
Now ask yourself, "How can I bring more joy?"

Acceptance is freedom.

changing from the inside out

Your inner state dictates how you perceive the world and how you act within it. How you sense the environment around you is dictated by your flow of energy through focus, breath, and movement.

Two parents can be at the same birthday party for their child, side by side, and have a completely different experience. While the kids are running randomly around, yelling and screaming, one parent, who is lighthearted and peaceful, can perceive fun, excitement, and enthusiasm, and the other, who is stressed, controlling, and agitated, can perceive absolute chaos. The same children's voices elicit joy, awe, and gratitude in one parent, and irritation and frustration in the other. Same environment, entirely different experience. These parents, because of their different inner states, will talk to their friends differently about the party, how it went, and if it was fun. Two people, two different states, two very different experiences, and ultimately two different realities.

The point is that if you want your reality to change, or you would like to enjoy what is happening in your environment, even if it feels stressful or chaotic, you must change your inner state first. What we call reality is created by your inner state of well-being and ultimately has nothing to do with your environment.

Multiply this simple birthday party example by every single event in your life, and you will quickly realize the value of being inwardly connected. Your inner well-being determines the quality of your life experiences now, in the past, and in the future. If this is the case, and your inner well-being is your greatest asset, what then becomes relevant in life?

What are the inner states that you regularly express throughout the week? Anger, sadness, happiness, joy, love, awe, peace, frustration, et cetera?

From these states, what are the internal stories that you tell yourself daily and most often? Life is beautiful, crazy, perfect, chaotic, tiring, energizing, abundant, lacking, et cetera?

How will you nurture your greatest asset, your inner well-being?

What is your most important physical, emotional, and mental practice that you can commit to?

My inner state is reflected in my outer reality.

getting our hands dirty

t makes me laugh to watch parents scrub their hands so vigorously, only to grab the handle of a door or shopping cart at a local retail store that has been handled by thousands. As if you can control the half a million bacteria that can fit on a pinhead. You must realize you are fighting a losing battle. Bacteria are everywhere. You cannot escape them. Nor would you want to. They are essential for life, and you would not be alive without them.

Ask yourself how many times you touch various objects in a day, each one of those objects containing trillions of bacteria. And you think washing your hands two hours ago makes a difference? Who told you these bacteria were so dangerous anyway? Did you know you have more bacteria than cells in your body?

This controlling of our environment is the great work of the ego. You must be conscious of the ego that says "Protect yourself at all times; be careful; don't take risks; be ever vigilant; your immune system isn't strong." There are some of you who are freaking out about this. Faulty belief systems and fear have been ingrained through the mindless numbing and fearmongering of a subculture that thrives on catastrophizing. You survived all the years of being a child, playing in the dirt without a care in the world. Where did that carefree freedom and innocence go? Don't you miss that little child in you, that spirit of freedom?

You also know that oftentimes it's not just fear of the germs—it's fear of being judged by others. We are communal and social beings. We want to be liked, loved, and accepted by others. Beyond the actual germs, it's important to take inventory on how much social and societal pressures and values are driving your thoughts, emotions, and behavior.

The frantic, obsessive nature over your children washing their hands and avoiding germs is, given the reality, amusing. For the sake of human sanity, and the future of our children, let's acknowledge and admit that there is no logical reason to be so scared.

Our culture has adopted these beliefs for no reason other than we've been fed this misinformation based on authorities being unconscious to the true nature of reality. Interestingly, with our obsession of trying not to be sick, we have turned into the sickest species on the planet. We want to play pretend, like we have control over bacteria or germs or our environment. When the truth is, there is no running away, and nowhere to go, because they are everywhere you are. Within and around you. Which is just the way it is designed to be.

Trying to eliminate bacteria is one of the most futile endeavors in parenting history.

Remember your childhood of playing outdoors, digging in the dirt, attending school, having mucky fingers, and putting them in your mouth hundreds if not thousands of times? Guess what? You are still here! It is not even fathomable to contemplate the magnitude of bacteria that you have and will be exposed to in your lifetime. At what point did we lose our common sense and the ability to allow ourselves to be okay with the planet's design? You are a living organism teamed up with other organisms for a symbiotic relationship. They are part of us. We are part of them.

Breathe in, breathe out . . . How'd the germs taste?

If we are all one, what if you chose to lead life with love, support, respect, and gratitude for other species and trust that their role is both necessary and valuable? Humans and other life-forms share the planet for a reason. We support one another's efforts in this game called life. We are connected with earth, nature, and all other life-forms on the planet. We need one another, and teaching our kids to be scared of dirt and bacteria and germs is teaching them a separatist and dualistic approach to life. Could our focus be setting them up for unnecessary paranoia and fear? Don't kids have enough to be concerned about these days?

When you and your children are connected to inner peace, you will each feel like you have more than enough to live in this world, and you will do so in harmony with all other creatures, big and small, and everything around you.

Take a moment and remember a few specific times
when you were a kid and got completely filthy.
Do you remember how much fun it was?
How you were okay after a good bath?

Who taught you that germs are bad?
Where did that belief come from, if it exists within you?

Could you take some time to go to the park, sit on the grass, get a little dirty, and experience the joy that can come from connecting to nature?

We are one with nature.

presence and force

Have you ever noticed how difficult it can be to get kids to do things or go places? Maybe it's trying to get them dressed or put on their shoes, but it just doesn't seem to be working. You feel angst inside of you, as your temper and emotions build when something is not going your way or not going according to plan.

As this emotion builds, you continue to stew, focusing on how no one is doing what you asked and life in this moment is not going the way you want it to. It's at this point of frustration that you disconnect from presence and focus more on what's not working.

As you continue to lessen your presence within your stressed reality, you feel a stronger urge to take matters into your own hands, as your ego looks for ways to control your emotions and experience. Your mind further gets away from you as you start thinking about how you haven't been heard or how your orders were not obeyed: "Didn't you hear what I said?" "Can't you follow some simple instructions?" "Just do what I say the first time!" Now the experience of a distorted reality enhances the "temperature" of the environment, and it feels like things are heating up.

You may start to behave in a childlike way yourself; you might speak in a louder voice, use aggressive or physical force, express anger and frustration; maybe you just explode to let off some steam! Understand, as your presence lessens, your force must increase. To make any type of change, even when it's something as simple as sitting down for supper or having the children come in from playing outside, we access force when we are not accessing presence. Then all of a sudden you find yourself yelling, screaming, scolding, punishing, and threatening. The little voice inside you is saying, "Change is happening now or else!"

We access force when we are not accessing presence.

All this drama is designed to snap you back into reality, to bring you back to the present moment, and to redirect your energy and focus. You can blame your kids for misbehaving or being crazy, or you can refocus with the experience and observe yourself. It's a call to connect, to pause, and to see what is really in front of you. It's not them who need the time-out. You need the time-out to get grounded and centered. Decompress. Clear your mind. Just for fun, go sit yourself in the corner and don't come out until you can behave with some grace.

As you become more attentive and aware and adhere to the call of more presence, the change you are looking for can happen with much less effort or force. Just a nudge, not a push. Just a whisper, not a shout. Just a look, or even just your presence, can make it happen. The energy involved in presence allows others to feel your safety and love, and therefore less force is required for guidance and change. The first step is to quickly acknowledge that whatever you are doing is clearly not working. What's plan B? Becoming more present.

The more present you are within yourself, the more unified you are with reality. The more unified with reality, the more you are flowing *with* life, instead of against it. Within the flow, you may find that there is a gentle guidance required, or even none at all. Part of you knows how to roll with the punches and go with the flow. It can be a seemingly effortless experience, unattached to outcomes, taking it as it comes, and living moment to moment. You know what this feels like, when things in life just click and work effortlessly. Simply imagine driving to a mall, hitting every green light, driving into a perfect parking spot, heading into the store, and grabbing the perfect shirt off the first rack and going to pay without a wait in line. That's flowing effortlessly. Another way to flow effortlessly is when you hit all the red lights, you can't find a parking spot, you can't find anything to wear, and there is a ten-person line when you do . . . and you laugh it off and remain poised and calm. The potential for flow lies in ourselves, not the circumstances we find ourselves in.

Discover the formula of presence for yourself, one that will rein you in when times get tough. When you are in presence, observe how much force is required, through your tone of voice, body, or emotions. Now observe when you are not present. See where your mind wanders, past or present, to allow this to occur. Draw your attention to the present situation and stay there, without fighting it, without trying to change it, and allow yourself to meet the reality, feel what is, and see how you move from reaction mode to more grace and ease.

Do you practice breath work regularly? Yoga?
Do you have a walking or hiking routine?

What will your formula for presence be?

All is well.

mother nature

I t's an uphill battle to raise healthy children if they are disconnected from nature. Mother Nature provides both adults and children alike a vitality that cement and concrete cannot. The further disconnected your children become from the natural world, the more interventions will be required to keep them well. The same goes for parents.

If your children are indoors all day, encased in bricks and mortar, anticipate listless or squirrelly, fidgety, agitated, or confused behavior. A sharp, aggressive personality is a classic description toward that of a caged and likely agitated animal. What shall we do with these kids who act like caged animals? What have we done with them in our culture to this point?

What happens to you when you are indoors for too long? What happens to you when you disconnect from nature? It's called cabin fever. Have you ever felt cooped up, not able to move or express your body or emotions or feel the freedom of the outdoors? What is your mood, and what do you feel like when you're stuck indoors, not able to move and breathe in a nurturing, natural environment? Between school, home, and indoor activities, imagine how much of the first twenty-five years of life are potentially spent disconnecting from nature.

How can children and parents connect with the vital life energy uniquely provided by nature? How can we add greater well-being and inner harmony? Nature assists in connecting the spirit and the physical body, in turn promoting more health while creating greater inner connection and peace. Nature assists in the healing process. You and your child are in a constant state of healing and repairing. We all need and deserve the opportunity to connect to this vitality and energy that Mother Nature can provide.

Make sure you and your family spend time experiencing the outdoors—a park, playground, or your own backyard. Just taking in the sounds, smells, and textures of nature. You don't have to do anything specific, just connecting with what is around you. The fresh air, sunshine, animals, and vegetation.

Commit to rolling around, playing outside, exploring the surroundings with your children, and the family dynamics will be enhanced, more well, and more healthy.

Write down how many hours you and your family connected outdoors this week and how many hours everyone was indoors. Contrast the two, and observe the emotions, moods, and energy that were felt within the house. Observe the effects of nature's wonder on your well-being.

Nature nurtures.

oneness

There is so much violence in the world. People disconnecting and dishonoring one another. Wars, bloodshed, and destruction are realities of life on our planet. We still do not see one another as part of one working system in the world. Instead we see one another separate in survival.

If we are to embrace peace, love, and connection as our future, then things need to change, and it starts early: with children.

Some of us have been encouraged to squash a harmless living bug for no reason at all, or see no potential consequence in doing so. For every action there is an equal and opposite reaction. How is a child to differentiate respect for one but not for another? They don't have the mental capacity to reason at an early age. Caring for the smallest of the living will translate to caring for the largest of the living. Kids have an innate, natural tendency toward unity and love. Respect for life is inherent. We often teach them disrespect.

When connecting with others and nature, the opportunity to

experience oneness is available. They see the people, bugs, worms, grass, trees, and dirt as different components of nature working together, and themselves as part of it all. They see and experience separateness and unity simultaneously.

Respect is taught through us holding the space for our children so they can trust and embrace this knowing. It is taught through how we talk about others with adults. It is taught through the ways we treat the earth. It is taught through holding open a door for another, or a kind gesture to let someone who is in a hurry go in front of us in a line. It is taught through how we talk with our kids one-on-one. Every interaction we have is another opportunity to teach our kids how to interact with other people and the environment. They must be allowed to explore their innate connection while we do our best to set the bar high. To embrace the unity within nature means we look at everything as having value.

Begin by teaching yourself about unity, respect, caring, and concern for all life-forms. This encourages kids to embrace what is already known. This action will extend far into the future by instilling compassion and empathy for all of life.

Remind yourself first to respect all things, as you may be the one who needs to reconnect. Then, as you live it you allow your kids to continue to grow with what they already know. Within our true essence we are all one.

To some, especially those brought up in a certain worldview of hierarchy, this concept may be a challenge. You may say, it's just a bug. It's just an insect. Yes, and it's showing them a paradigm of respect and love for all beings. It is important to be congruent in what we say and how we act.

How do you teach your kids about respect? How are you the mentor?

*How could you be more congruent when it comes to respect,
from the smallest to the largest life-forms?*

———————————

**My consciousness grows
in love for all living things.**

flow

Remember as a kid how hard it was to swim upstream? Remember the effort it took to go up the slide, not down? Remember how much easier it was to float down a river?

You know those days where you tell your friends how tough it was to be a parent? A day where the house was a mess, the kids were fighting, and it felt like nothing was getting accomplished? How everyone wasn't listening, how everyone was misbehaving, how draining the day was?

You were trying to swim against the current.

Within life, within us, within the spirit of a child flows a rhythm; and rhythms go where rhythms need to go. The rhythms flow to the next experience and the next learning. Do you think you are powerful enough to disrupt these rhythms? Do you think you can compete with the river? Try competing with the force of a bowel movement ready to discharge! Impossible! This competing is a tremendous source of suffering. We call this "trying." We try desperately at times to stop the flow of energy and repress it. This stifling takes a tremendous amount of mental and physical energy. Why? Because you are trying to control the rhythms that are far beyond your control.

Some of you will ask, "How do I protect them?" or "How do I teach them if I just flow with life?" It's so impractical and impossible to do in many circumstances. Great, let's continue.

Have you ever observed how effortless it is for a bird to fly with the wind? It is the most energy-efficient way to fly. The bird surrenders.

Children are the wind. You are the bird. Fly with them.

A flower is supported by soil and grows toward the sun. Again, like the bird flying with the wind, it does so because this is the most effortless way to thrive and optimizes its chances to flourish.

Your children are no different. They have needs to grow and to live. Their rhythms, regardless of convenient timing, will move and shift toward where they need to go to thrive.

They are the flower. You are the soil. Let them follow the sun.

Stop trying, stop controlling, be present with them, and surrender.

They are tying a shoe. Instead of jumping in to teach them how to do it faster, sit there and wait. They will feel your support and call upon you when they want help. If they are struggling, wait and watch as though you are watching a movie. Stay out of the way until life calls you.

With this approach, the one of being fully present, you are able to respond to their needs. This will bring greater ease for you, more joy throughout the day, and fulfillment in caring for your little ones. There is a great sense of freedom that can come from experiencing the rhythms and inspirations of flowing with the river. Presence. Awareness. Engagement.

You see, this flow with life, this dance with what is . . . it's practice. It's practice for you to work with a part of you that is underpracticed. Most parents want to control every experience. And what I'm encouraging is to practice the style of relaxing, of flowing, of not having to get in the way all the time. You are important, of course. But don't make yourself more important than what's happening in the moment. Sometimes staying out of the way and flowing with what is, is as beneficial for them as it is you.

When your kids are pulling you one way, notice your initial response of resistance.

Why are you resisting?

What version of you is resisting?

How can you surrender?

———————————

I feel the ease and flowing within.

feel the pain

I f your kids get a cut, have them feel it. Don't immediately stitch it and bandage it to avoid the pain. That's what most parents do. Bandaging a cut quickly to avoid the pain is so symbolic of what our culture does in life. If they are dismissed from the team, let them feel it. Don't try to fix it or save them.

Denying someone the ability to feel pain, whether physical or emotional, is denying them the opportunity for growth and for change.

If our kids go on a binge of foods they are not used to, it's important for them to realize that the body is smart and giving them feedback through a sore tummy. How else will they learn?

Teach your kids to embrace pain. Get them curious. Don't have them scared of a sore tummy or a little cut. Let them feel it. Let them feel every bit of it. Because if they get used to feeling it, they won't be intimidated in life when they experience pain. They will feel it and make better and wiser decisions. They will learn how to harness the discomfort and not make every attempt to avoid it by popping pills or denying it's there. They will learn to face it and embrace it. They will learn to connect with the pain, yell and scream out loud, release and resolve the energy.

Let them learn and explore the possibilities of connecting with pain so they can make the changes necessary in life when life throws curveballs. If we don't learn to connect with ourselves during unpleasant times, we get stuck in ruts and feel frustrated and irritated.

You may not be there for them when they are thirty years old to save them from the pains in life. In fact, you can't be, so why do you think you need to save them right now? It's training ground for real life! It is right now that will train them for when they are thirty.

Be there in support and love, but not to save them. Coach them to feel and breathe with the pain, whatever it may be. If they are frustrated with their school work and on the brink of tears, let them feel the emotions that arise. If they are mad at a friend for an insult, let them feel it through a gentle, loving, and silent hug. Don't try to coach them to not feel it. Don't get them in their head. Get them to tell you what it feels like inside. Help them to make the connection, to acquire healthy strategies and skills that will enable them to deal with a challenge regardless of its source or origin.

Awakening comes with feeling the experience and all that life has to offer. The joys and the pains, the bumps, bruises, and victories, the entire range of human experience, not just the ones that are comfortable or enjoyable.

As adults know, life is composed of all colors of the rainbow. Allow your kids to experience life with its pains and pleasures, and don't limit their exposure to what you think they should feel.

What if the next time they got injured or disappointed you helped them to feel their pain? What would that type of support look like?

How would you have to breathe, move, think, or feel in order to not try to be a rescuer?

**I hold the space of love
to nurture my child.**

innate potential

ave we forgotten about what we are made of?

When it comes to our kids, we go through a lot of pain and heartache unnecessarily. When faced with any challenge, be it health, behavior, family, friends, or academics, we lose trust that things will turn out.

We forget about who we are and what we are made of. We trust more in outside interventions to create change than we do in the very core of what we are made of. We trust a pill to work its magic more than the inborn wisdom that created us.

As well for our children, we suffer as parents when watching our kids struggle with health or life because we have forgotten what they are made of.

What organizes a flower to grow from a seed, to a bud, to a flower?

What organizes you from a sperm and egg into a living, breathing, thinking adult?

When we humble ourselves to this divine organizing intelligence, we surrender ourselves to that special something that is at work in our life, far beyond what we can imagine. We take it for granted that this intelligence is working for us twenty-four hours a day, seven days a week. This intelligence is there to run every facet of our body, millions upon millions of jobs per second. We eat; intelligence digests. We exercise; intelligence pumps blood. We work; intelligence moves us and allows us to think. Every single moment of our life, intelligence is working for us to heal and re-create itself in a healthy way.

So this brings us to our kids. Do we as parents trust this superior, incomprehensible intelligence? Because the very second something goes "wrong," we panic. We go through our day taking intelligence for granted. Then when a fever comes, or a cold, or a headache, we think we know better than this billion-year-old intelligence. We get frazzled, helpless, and powerless.

The human mind takes over and says, *I know best, and I must try to control.* It is when we are in a state of fear that we make decisions against our intuition and better logic.

The idea with health and well-being is so simple. The more this inborn intelligence is able to express itself, the greater health expression you and your children will experience. How can we free up this intelligence so it can operate fully? Unwind and release your physical and mental blocks. Build trust for you and for life. Through your actions you pass this trust on to your children.

Once you trust this intelligence, life gets fun, there is less fear, and you begin to look at the world in a more trusting way. Your health and well-being grow.

*What are some ways that you can engage your child
to embrace and feel confident in their inner potential?*

*What are some things you may have to remove
to help your child flourish even more?*

———————————

I have all I require to be well.

the joy of movement

Children inherently have a body sense, only to lose it. This is why playing and being active for a lifetime is critical to physical and mental well-being. Spirit expressed through the body is youthful vitality. As you age, it becomes more imperative to go inward, to connect, to move and reawaken your body.

The more disconnected you are from your body, the more disconnected and distorted you are from reality. Reality is a natural flow of energy willing to mold to your deepest desires. When you are connected with your body, you are connected to spirit. When you are connected with your rhythms, you are connected to life. When you are feeling fragmented in thought, ideas, confusion, lack of contentment, or not taking care of yourself, this is a sign of disconnection and distortion.

The body is the conduit between your inner and outer worlds. The body is how you see the world. It feeds your brain with the information from your environment. So your response to the environment is directly dependent upon the flexibility and ease and fluidity of the body. Embodied practices are a great way to keep the family well.

What activities can you encourage for your family that are fun and that allow everyone to feel the flow and natural ease of their body?

What signs does your child show you that they are being too cooped up and not active enough?

When do you notice that they are less anxious and more settled and grounded?

_____

I move, therefore I am.

your mirror

magine that every day, there was a video camera on you. This video camera was hooked up to a television station that broadcasted your every move the entire day. Every day. Every week. Every month. Every year. The reason for this? You were chosen to teach the world how to live by the highest standards of morals and ethics, attitudes and behaviors, moods and temperament, and apply these principles to everyday living.

The world would watch you meticulously, noting all you were being and doing.

A channel just on you.

How would you behave? What would be your approach to life? Your level of energy and enthusiasm? Your language? Your conversations? Your moods? Your actions? Your hygiene? Your clothes? Your walk? Your focus?

Your children watch you, emulate you, and mirror you. They are your reflection.

If you are curious as to what you look and sound like, both in the expressed and unexpressed parts of you, look no further than your children. They will show you everything you do and don't do, say and don't say. They are the video being played back to you for your viewing pleasure. They will graciously show you your most common moods, emotions, attitudes, actions, and views on life. Imagine a direct feedback loop for your most common way of being. How beautiful. How revealing.

I recently consulted a woman who was being challenged by her "mouthy daughter." She thought I was going to give her advice on how to change her child's behavior so that she would be more respectful and obedient. Instead, I asked her when the last time she herself was mouthy. She burst out laughing. All day she was bantering back and forth with her boss on a project she wasn't happy with. She was being cocky, rude, and what would appear to her boss as being "mouthy." We both had a good laugh. She saw my point. I asked her why she was being mouthy. She said because her boss wasn't listening to her point of view about the project and was trying to bully her into doing something she was against. Again, we shared a humbling and humorous realization—and a powerful insight.

So you can curse the channel, or you can use it as feedback to refine and improve yourself, your attitudes, your behaviors, and your life. You can reject, or you can accept. You can fight, or you can laugh. You can get moody, or you can gratefully endure the feedback and create a better way of being—an evolved version, one who inspires and raises the bar for yourself and your children. Are you enjoying the channel that you are watching?

You are watching yourself. You are not separate from your children.

You are wildly connected. As you go through your day, observe their actions, listen to them talking, or watch their way of being, and see the profound influence you have had on them.

This is not to be forgotten, because you have been unconsciously influencing them each and every day. Next time, instead of blowing a gasket or flying off the handle, look deep into their eyes and see yourself playing back to you.

What if you centered your life and actions around the top five attributes that you would want your child to see? What would they be?

Write them down and see in your mind's eye how your day might be if you lived life with these five attributes.

My children are my reflection.

let go of "success"

Children want to experience connection, love, and safety. They want to learn how the world works and express a freedom and flexibility as new things are attempted. A loved child is a happy child, living every day full of life, feeling safe to explore through all its infinite possibilities and adventures.

It is so unfortunate to see parents place intense pressure on their children to be "successful" in all they do. From sports to academics, we have become an all-in society, where if the child shows an interest, we structure them quickly for optimal success and achievement.

If the only thing children need is love, what are we doing putting so much pressure on them? Why are their schedules packed to the hilt? It's not fun for anyone, least of all our children, and we know it. Yet we decide to continue on, being lulled to a cultural dream, and think this is how life should look.

Is this as good as it gets for our kids? Being tossed from activity to activity, getting them dressed in the car, eating on the run, hours spent in a competition they may not even like?

What are we willing to sacrifice in our family life for the never-ending desire for our kids to be highly successful? Don't we say that we just want our kids to be happy and healthy?

Allow your child to guide the next step. Are you really listening to whether they love something? Are you watching their facial expressions, their tone, their posture, how they talk about it, or their level of energy with the activity? Are you taking inventory of the feedback from your child, or are you too busy cheering? Are they telling you they don't want to do it? Are they showing signs of burnout?

Surrender. Drop your expectations of what you think your child should do or like. If you want to give your children a variety of activities, release the attachment to results, achievements, and successes.

Let them have fun. They will gravitate to their natural loves, and excel and be disciplined in those. You do not need to teach love of anything. When they have a love, one inspired from within, they exhibit a natural discipline, a by-product of their love being cultivated and supported . . . until they decide to change what they love and what inspires them.

Oftentimes, parents get fixated on one activity because they did it or loved it as a child. What if you let your child explore their interests and let them guide you to the next step? What if you allow their rhythms to show you what they are interested in?

Connect with your child, not with what they do. When you are connected to your child's desires and not your hopes and dreams, you will allow them to be and do anything with open acceptance and love.

Embrace the role of being their tour guide to life. Show them all there is to enjoy. The tour guide doesn't say what to love on the tour. He doesn't get excited about some things and *Embrace the role of being their tour guide to life.* not others. He gets excited about all the attractions equally, and the tourist gets to choose what they want to focus on and explore. The guide doesn't care; he is just there to guide.

That is what you are as a parent. You are a guide, without an attachment to what your child loves or focuses their attention on. To accept this magnificent role as a tour guide of all life has to offer is a great responsibility in and of itself.

Pay attention. Be aware. Allow them to discover their own far places to explore and let them enjoy the adventure.

With this balanced and neutral focus on your child's activities, you will have no attachment to or care what your child loves or does. You will just celebrate that your child is loving life.

How do you define success for your child?
How does it reflect the rich picture of life you want them to experience?

I allow my children to soulfully grow and follow their dreams.

the myth of fitting in

You ou may feel that your child has to be like other children. You may feel inadequate if your child isn't "meeting" societal and cultural norms. You try extra hard to have your child match and meet the "expectations" of researchers, scientists, teachers, and doctors.

How much pain might you cause yourself and your children when you compare and contrast them to others? How tiring is this for you? Do you realize that your ego is the only thing that cares about their timely development?

The ego focuses on timing, decides what's right and wrong, perceives your children as delayed or advanced, deems them wise or stupid, or labels them slow or fast, underdeveloped or overdeveloped. The ego assesses everything in duality, black-and-white. The ego is all about performance, time lines, and "stages of growth." We evaluate our children using our obsession with rules.

It's time to chill.

What if the rule was that there were no rules?

Have you ever planted a garden? It takes time to grow. You do have to plant the seed, but you can't rush the process. No matter how hard you try, you just cannot control or expedite the growth of a living system. Each seed will develop in its unique time, have its own distinct appearance, shape, and color. No two will be identical. No two will grow or bloom at precisely the same time. Some seeds grow fast, some slow. Some flowers bloom bright, and others linger softly in the background. Some flowers spread their seeds; others do not. Some are loud and colorful, others dull and subtle. Some die early. Some live longer. Some will be consistent and predictable, while others, unpredictable. Some require specific, detailed care, while some are autonomous and independent. Some flowers grow no matter how bad or good the weather; others are easily influenced by the slightest turbulence. Some excel in the sun, some in the rain. Some need cool temperatures; some need hot or tropical ones.

What we do know is that every flower is different, grows uniquely and in its own time. It is so easy to accept this fundamental truth of nature: that everything has a unique fingerprint concerning time, growth, and development. The same holds true for children.

Why, then, is it so difficult for an adult to apply this very same principle? Why do we have such a hard time accepting the differences in development, growth, timing, and their unique expressions of life? Yes, there are ranges and milestones, but no two children will ever be exactly the same. Why do we create suffering in our children by imposing expectations, comparing them to their peers or, worse, other generations before them? If we accept that all children are unique and have their own masterful blueprint in this world, then why are we comparing them?

How do we as parents fully accept the unique and individualistic nature of each child as living, breathing, moving beings? How do we fully accept that they too follow the rules of nature? Why do we worry, contrast, and compare?

We surrender to a garden with the trust that nature takes care of things. When we tend to a garden, it's relatively easy to accept when a particular flower has a bit of a slow start, while another seems as though it's thriving. We don't reward or ridicule flowers for their development; we accept what is. It's how nature works and how living things grow. Nature works on perfect timing and perfect rhythm. So do our children.

Machines are the opposite. They are programmed to work the same, produce the same, and be predictable. Children are not machines. They are living, dynamic beings of spirit.

So enough comparing. Let children grow and develop with love. Do like we do with the flowers in a garden. Our job entails watering, tending to, and nurturing. Your child has his or her own path of life, their own unique rhythms and timing that is beyond the understanding of our educated minds.

Each child has a special intangible force that drives their life, just like you have. Ease up a little. A parent exists to tend and nurture the soul of a child. We are not there to force or expect them to meet our standards. That approach does not work.

Trying too hard is a reflection of fears that they will not be enough and that we are failures as parents. Your children are more than enough right this moment, just the way they are. They are just as they need to be. Judgment will lead down a path of distress.

They may be developing slowly now and pick up the pace, or they may be fast and slow down. Or they may never slow down or may never speed up. Who cares? They will ultimately find their place in the world, which is out of your control anyway. Step away and let nature unfold life so you as a parent can surrender and enjoy the process.

Trust that you will know when to nudge, when to ease off, when to speak, and when to remain silent. Listen to your heart; observe their rhythms. They will guide you. Just stop talking, and listen. They are whispering the messages every day in 1,001 different ways.

How often do you genuinely express gratitude for these little seedlings that you have created and for the very uniqueness they are? Remember, one day they too will be adults wanting to give their gifts to the world.

Provide them with the freedom to learn about who they are and why they are here. Know in your heart that they have unlimited potential and that everything unfolds in its right time and right place and right rhythm.

You sprinkle the water, provide the nutrients, be the sun, and just let them grow.

What's one area where you can lighten up and let go of expectations?

What's one area where you intuitively know you need to challenge your child to rise to a greater level?

Ease, flow, and let them grow.

resist labels

Why do we label our kids?

The surest way to get certainty is to label something. Why is he sad? Because he is depressed. Why is she mad? Because she's a grouch. Why did he do that? Because he is selfish. Why don't they listen? Because they are sensitive, or oppositional, or otherwise deficient in some way.

Labeling people is a method used by the mind to help someone feel certain and safe. It gives us a false sense of control while allowing us to identify and "understand" situations or circumstances. It is used when we are functioning from fear-based consciousness. When we get scared, the mind says, *I need to fixate reality into a solid box so I can understand it and feel safe.* It's part of the ego structure of being human. The mind thinks it knows, therefore it feels secure. Nowadays, anytime we feel the discomfort of uncertainty, anytime we are feeling like we don't know enough, we run to the computer to search for certainty.

Labeling is usually done under fear and stress, and generally speaking, the decisions that come from a place of fear are seldom best in the long run. Most decisions made in fear are going to have very different consequences from those made with love.

So what happens when we take this labeling idea and apply it to our kids? When our kids are acting outside our comfort zone, we tend to want to label.

In our holistic practice, for example, we look at anywhere between six and ten major contributing factors to understand why a child may have difficulty concentrating. They don't have a mental illness or disorder. They have a brain and body that are uninterested in sitting still and focusing on what the adult deems important. We need to look at behavior not through the lens of a "problem" that needs to be fixed but rather as a process that can be potentially improved upon.

Labeling comes from the disconnected and suffering mind. It is a way we attempt to feel empowered from outside of ourselves. It's a way to deal with adversity so that you don't have to pay attention to the inner cues, needs, or uncomfortable rhythms.

Having children diagnosed is a way of feeling safe and regaining a sense of control. It's not to say it is bad; it is just a strategy to gain certainty. We are trying to cope with feeling scared and helpless.

If you were stuck on an island with your child, you would figure it all out and accept them for who they are. Figuring out what is "wrong" with a child is ingrained in how many of us were taught to handle the stress and uncertainty of an experience or situation. But there are other approaches as well.

It is through insecurities and fears that we give kids these labels that potentially stay with them for a lifetime. We need to be careful about labeling our children and accepting the labels imposed on them by others, even with the best of intentions.

How often do you label yourself or your child?

If you were to look at them as an evolving painting or piece of art,
what labels have you placed on them that need to be let go?
Do you see them as sweet, sassy, cocky, fun, hilarious
and put more emphasis on one of them?
Watch how you have potentially formed labels without even realizing it.

I release the labels
and embrace all their parts.

life is a verb

nstead of labels, try thinking in verbs. Nothing in our true reality is static or frozen. Only the mind's concepts are frozen. All of our trillions of cells are constantly active and in motion. Nothing is stationary. Life is motion; motion is life. The truth is, everything can be a verb—a word used to describe an action.

What if you used verbs to describe what you or your kids were expressing or experiencing? An easy transition might sound like, "My child is fevering right now." "My child is coughing right now." There is motion and movement in those statements.

Your essence is dynamic and free. Anything is changeable in the next moment; this is the "unattached" changeability of reality. So if we say our child has "a fever" or has "a cough," there is a freezing of reality. As a result, you will move into suffering because it appears to the mind that there is no end.

On the other hand, saying "right now he is fevering" or "right now he is coughing" gives power to the true and mercurial nature of reality, which is energy in motion. The words *right now* are key because the mind will interpret the reality as temporary, not permanent.

This slight shift in perception allows for change and movement and greater acceptance so reality can shift. When we take this approach, you keep energy in motion and keep yourself moving with life. You will then find and discover the people, approaches, tools, or techniques that assist you in working and moving through a situation.

Teach your children that they are a verb. Talk to yourself like you are a verb. You are energy in motion, fluid, and changeable from moment to moment. No matter the situation or circumstance, energy can alter itself and shift in a new direction because that is what energy does. Energy is what you are, and energy is consciousness. Energy moves, changes, and transforms.

Think of a time a year ago that was stressful,
and it seemed so solid and real at the time—what was it?

How has the memory of it changed now?

———————

Life is motion; motion is life.

self-love

Your kids want you to be well. They want you around for a long time. They want you to have energy and to be wild, crazy, fun, and loving. How can you do that if you don't take care of yourself?

In an airplane, they always instruct us to place our own oxygen mask on first, before helping anyone else. This is because you are not nearly as effective if you are not taking care of you.

How are you supposed to be that fun-loving parent when you don't take time to pamper yourself, get enough exercise and outdoor activity, get adjusted, have a massage, laugh until your belly hurts, eat nutritious food, or even take a shower!

Your children are watching your every move. They see you haven't combed your hair in two days. They see and feel when you are dragged down and worn-out. They notice if you rarely smile or almost never laugh.

They also see when you are alive, vibrant, well, content, peaceful, joyful, and abundant in energy. They love this version because it matches who they are.

When they are not feeling enough of your vibrant energy, they will find a way to wake you up. They will bring a competing energy to you. Maybe they will burp in your face, yell and scream, slap you on the rear end, or pull your hair. Something to shake you up and allow you to tap into that vibrant energy. They are your shot of adrenaline, your espresso-like stimulation, there to nudge you, take your mind off your worries and woes. They are miniature rays of sunshine.

Only you can raise the standard you set for your well-being. How well you nurture yourself determines your experience both in the present and future. You are also influencing generations to come with your habits and practices. Personal care is showing your children that looking after yourself is important. Beyond that, your kids want you to be well, and your habits will become their habits.

What standards have you currently set for yourself?

Consider when you are at your highest standard:
How are you dressed and what do you wear?
How do you do your hair? How do you keep your house?
How do you keep your work station? What do you cook?
How can you bring this mind-set to your everyday experiences?

**I love and care for myself often,
because I am worth it.**

right now

The question is, how many more moments are you going to let slip away? How many more times are you going to think about other stuff, instead of focusing your complete and undivided attention on what is right in front of you?

Do you want to look back on your years and wonder where the hell they went, or do you want to experience everything life has to offer you right now?

Children are so excited to show you how much fun life can be; to show you what they are learning; to share with you their art, a leaf, a drawing, a climb, a tumble, a tree; the simple everyday things adults take for granted; the very things we tend to lose appreciation for, the very things we dismiss as ordinary or trivial. These are the magical moments we let pass us by as parents: the moments of reality.

How can we engage in these magical moments? Be attentive in the present moment. Be "right here, right now."

This is the paradigm shift so many of us need to embrace to resolve many of our troubles. We tend to bypass the magical moments in exchange for drifting our attention to "the grass on the other side of the fence," which is of course "greener" than our current reality. Always more peaceful, more organized, less busy, more serene, and more fulfilling.

Instead, we are busy in our heads wishing for anything but our current reality. Wandering thoughts of a vacation, an incoming text, emails, and a new wardrobe. Focusing our thoughts on anything our mind can try to grasp that is not in the present moment with our children. We have occupied our time with mental wandering in exchange for living.

What are your most common go-to vices that distract you from the present moment? List your top three.

There is nothing else but right now.

practicing presence

What will life deal us in order for us to be fully awake and aware? At times we all need wake-ups in our life to bring us present and to connect us to the moment. Those wake-ups are designed to get us more real with greater depth of authenticity.

If we stay more awake and make a conscious effort to do so, we build more resilience for times of challenge, and life becomes more effortless and more magical.

There is a time to think about your future. There is a time to dream. There is a time to work and plan. There is a time to do all these things, but it's not when you are with your children. When you drift off in the presence of your kids, it's time lost that you'll never get back.

Most parents think they are present. This is an illusion. Just because you are physically there does not mean you're being present. How many times do you need to have your attention grabbed? How many times have you read the same page of their favorite book, amazed that they have memorized it and you haven't? They are so focused. You are not. While you may believe or have convinced yourself that you're spending quality time with them, you're not in tune with the experience of the moment. Let's get there now.

Focus on what your child is saying. Place your hand on their arm when they talk with you. Totally immerse yourself in the experience and embrace it like it will be the last time they ever talk to you, or show you a statue they made, or swing on the swing set. Concentrate your focus. Claim your time together. Fully share your child's magic moments. This is active, real-life meditation at its best.

Being present takes practice outside of when you are with your children. What practices are you doing to help hone your skills of presence and focus?

How long can you dedicate per day to these practices? Now is the time where you can put it in your schedule.

Presence is my purpose.

wanting

You know how tiring it gets when your kids ask you over and over again for new things, more toys, and more stuff? In your heart, you know that it's not going to bring them happiness and that it's something that will never end. They are there to remind you of this most critical awareness, that more stuff will only draw your awareness away from the beauty of what is most important. The "wanting" game draws us away from real presence and connection.

"I'll be happy when . . ." is a fascinating game the mind plays to stay busy. "Wanting" is the mind's way of controlling and believing that happiness is just around the corner. We lose connection.

Micromanaging your environment, by saying things such as "Once I get this room clean I will be so happy!" or "Once I lose ten pounds I will feel so happy," is the mind's way of staying in "wanting" mode. If it's not the room or the pounds, it will be something else.

We want to become aware of, and acknowledge, that there will always be a longing and desire of the mind to think that life will be better when the circumstances change. In this wanting, you will never find peace. The illusion is that once you get what you want, you will be happy. You won't. There will always be another want. Wanting pulls you from being present. When there is no presence, there is no peace. When there is peace, presence, and love, you are full; there is no void, and therefore, there is no wanting.

You already see this in your kids. They want a toy, then they get it, they play with it, then they want more. And so the cycle of wanting begins.

How has "wanting" ruled your world in some areas of life?
Do you see this in your kids too?
What can you do to quiet the wanting and reconnect to the here and now?

I am full, whole, and complete.

change for change's sake

How many of your thoughts throughout the day are focused on what needs to change? Your child needs a haircut, it's time the pacifier comes out, there's a cup in the wrong place, the chair cushion is crooked, there are raisins on the floor, the kid's teeth aren't brushed, or their shirt is too big.

Can we just pause and take a breath? Can we look at our kids for the amazing light they are? Can we see beyond our own obsessive and neurotic desire to have things perfect and see the perfection in them?

Catch yourself and be mindful of your inner chatter.

How many times throughout the day are you wanting to change something about your family? Are their shoes on the wrong feet, or are they wearing mismatched clothes? Do they need a better jacket or warmer socks?

Pay attention to how many times you feel the need to change something, even if it's just a little. Maybe you say, "Oh, honey, that shirt and pants don't match," or "Are you sure you tried your best to color in the lines?" How many times must we obsessively micromanage? This may be done repeatedly throughout the day, with very few of these changes actually making a difference or being relevant. Changing something for change's sake is all about control. It's toxic. This creates stress instead of peace.

What if today you let your kids be exactly as they are,
without changing a thing? What would that look like?

How much self-restraint would it take
to consciously allow life to look messy?

I replace judgment with acceptance.

the future

How do we release baggage from the past? It's a weight that you carry around with you, like rocks in a backpack. It can be an event that happened two decades ago, or yesterday. It's paralyzing and will keep you stuck and chained to an energy that can and must be released.

It's difficult to be peaceful and to stay present with anyone, especially your children, when you are holding on to grudges, events, or circumstances rooted in the past.

You may not realize it. Your kids can feel and see the tension that you carry as it keeps you angry, bitter, or guilt-ridden instead of being your authentic, joyful self. Let's explore letting go of the baggage from our past.

Think of a swinging trapeze artist for a moment. He is swinging on one swing, hands chalked up and gripping the swing tight, muscles bulging, body flexible, back and forth in the air. You can see him gaining momentum, with the sense of anticipation building.

When you are watching him, you are excited because at some point you know that he is going to let go of the swing. So here is a question for you. Is he building his focus to let go of the swing, or is he building up enough momentum to grab on to the other swing?

If he was focused on letting go, he would just let go and fall. The probability of his success to grab hold of the other swing would be minimal. Interestingly, he is not focused on letting go but rather focused on what he will need to do in the present moment to be able to grab hold of his target.

How does this apply to you? How many times have people told you to just let go of something? Just forget about it. Just let the past be the past. Unfortunately, it doesn't work that way.

If you focus on letting go, you stay focused on the past and stay in fear. We need to have presence within us, and a compelling future to grab hold of while using courage, determination, and focus. Maybe you want to experience something as simple as more love and gratitude or being more present.

When the trapeze artist decides to grab hold of the other swing, he reaches for the future, which results in letting go of the past. When you decide to grab hold of a compelling future, your past baggage falls away. The trapeze artist knows what his target is while focusing diligently on the present moment and what needs to be done right now to get there.

You believe that you need to let go of your past. You can't. It is part of you. But you can accept that you experienced the pain, anger, fear, guilt, or shame and use that awareness to redefine yourself, your life, and your actions.

So much so that you become grateful for their happenings and they become fuel for your growth. The past becomes irrelevant to your new way of thinking, actions, and focus. You can view your past as a gift of experiences that catapults you to a much greater version of you, or you can view it as an anchor that keeps you a victim and a prisoner of the energy of the past. Which do you choose?

What new, compelling future do you need to create to keep you moving forward, not backward?

What are three things life is calling from you to grab ahold of and move forward?

I awaken to unlimited potential.

feeling our feelings

Why would we want our children to connect with how they feel?

Well, millions of people are feeling stuck in life; stuck in their monkey minds. As a society, we have become disconnected from recognizing the importance of our feelings and their use for creating change. Thought, on the other hand, has been placed at the top of the hierarchy and has become the main tool to guide us in decision-making.

Stop reading for a moment. Place your free hand on your chest and breathe into it. Slowly, inhale and exhale, feeling the rise and fall of your chest, the rhythm, the breath, the energy. Now close your eyes and continue to focus on how it feels beneath your hand for a few moments. This is feeling.

Perhaps you want to yell and scream many times throughout the day but instead decide to toxically hold it in and say, "Everything is fine"; say, "I am cool, calm and collected, and peaceful." Hogwash.

That emotion will catch up with you, and then some. You must connect and release, or the withholdings will clog the mind.

Feeling is what people avoid. Many believe that feeling, this calming, connective act, is less valuable than thinking. Feeling has the ability to be an amazing way to change or transform. The times you've made significant change in your life occurred when you connected with a new feeling and emotional sensation—one that was strong enough for you to take action. Yet, instead of using what works, you automatically revert to rationalizing when you are trying to create change. Using this rote approach, you stay stuck. Emotions get you moving, and learning to tap into them is a wellspring for life.

This is why it is imperative that you nurture your child in a way that demonstrates how to connect with their feelings. A simple question of "What do you feel about this?" instead of "What do you think about this?" works for many. And when your child feels sad, sit with it. Make space. The most limiting words a child can hear are "Don't cry."

As parents we must embrace the emotional ranges of our children and fully embrace them without judgment. These ranges will be so useful for our children later in life if they feel confident enough to feel and express them.

Come up with ways that you can help your child explore new ranges of emotions. Maybe you pick emotions out of a hat and play a game to act them out. Maybe you make the sounds of different emotions.

The idea is to break the stigma of expressing only the "good" emotions and embrace all emotions as useful in life.

There are no good or bad emotions.

There are no good or bad emotions. They are purely emotions. And all emotions are useful in different circumstances and situations.

By embracing all parts of yourself, and showing your children all parts of themselves are important, you can embrace wholeness.

What games can you play with the family to practice expressing greater ranges of emotions? Which emotions do you think you will be most uncomfortable expressing?

———————

**To express wholeness,
I must embrace all parts of me.**

be love

They say that love moves mountains. How many mountains have you moved lately? You know what I mean. Giving love can be a challenging task in the midst of chaotic living. You may say that you give love all the time. The concept of love, maybe, but the real, authentic practice of love requires more presence and awareness than what you are used to.

We are often too absorbed in "doing." So much of our time is spent in our head and not our heart. Don't be too critical though; it's easy to slip into the unconscious patterns of everyday living—those patterns where our mind wanders on how to change things and make them better; how to be happier, healthier, more fit; how to lose weight, steal some alone time; how to make more money; and how to better organize life.

Do you realize how much time is spent—no, wasted—on fantasizing about how to make life different? This pattern of "non-present daydreaming" does not include love.

Since love is fundamental to the child's experience, the question becomes for the modern parent, how authentic are you? In the fast-paced world in which we currently live, how plausible is it really?

If so many parents are functioning in this daydreaming reality, leading stressful and chaotic lives, how is any child going to feel authentic love if their parent is focused on everything but being present to give? I know you are doing a lot for your child, but what about just being love and giving that to them? It's time to deeply evaluate how you love. It's time to compassionately check in with yourself, to look at your level of presence when you are with your child and what your version of love looks like.

When you say "I love you" to your child, notice what your next thought is. How badly does your ego require a response? Is there an expectation of return? Do you need acknowledgment or a reply? You didn't need a reply when they were a newborn. I'll bet if you don't hear them return your sentiments, something inside of you starts to speak up. If they don't say "I love you too," how does that make you feel? To the ego, no response now creates a void that needs to be filled. You persist, maybe get a little louder, try to be more convincing, and repeat yourself until you get the response you need.

When you provide pure love, there is no need for the child to return the words. They just absorb it and respond according to how they feel in the moment. They aren't thinking that you are going to take it personally if they don't say "I love you" back. They are just kids. It is only your ego that demands validation and therefore needs to hear those words reciprocated. The same goes for your relationship with your partner. It's the same egoism merry-go-round. What if the agendas are dropped and you were truly in touch with what is precisely motivating you?

You might say "I love you" to your children when they are suffering from a fall or scrape, without a need for return. You could say "I love you" when they are ill or in a weakened state. You have no trouble saying "I love you" without a need for a return then. Why? Because this is true, authentic love. Take a look at how you say those words when your children are well. Do you really want them to know it, in that moment, or are you just saying it to get love, to hear your child proclaim their love for you?

When you say "I love you," ask yourself where it's coming from. Are you saying it through the mind or through your entire being? Are you saying it with a tone of purity and innocence so that they are able to feel what love is in that moment? Bringing your spirit and heart into expressing love is an embodied process, not a monotone delivery courtesy of the mind. The mind has no character and no emotion. The mind is thoughts.

Your child will feel any incongruence behind your words. Don't be fooled. They know when you are heartfelt and selfless, and they also know when you are looking for a return. Don't be surprised if you find yourself repeating the words over and over; chances are you are not being authentic with your embodied communication of love and your child is calling you on it! If you catch yourself doing that with your children, you most likely do that with your partner and other loved ones.

Since getting love is a need of our child self, it is a pattern that potentially runs throughout adult life if we are not bringing attention and awareness to it.

Waking from our child patterns takes awareness and persistence. Use words of love only when you are authentically being love. Don't say "I love you" if you are looking for a return. Be love. Let them feel you. Let them feel the rhythm of love flow through you and around you. They will return a coy smile, or soften, or delight you with a spontaneous unexpected return of something magical. Maybe words, maybe not; it doesn't matter.

Say "I love you" until you know they have been moved, that they have felt your sincerity and presence. Get close, hold them tight, and let them feel you. Embody love for them. Show them how love is really done and how love really feels.

What if you were to go in for a hug without the need or expectation
for a return hug? How do you think your mind would respond?
How open can your heart stay without receiving one back?
It's important to observe this part of the mind.
It's the part of mind that interferes with the experience of true love.

I am love.

honoring the present moment

L ove is the center of our beings. Loving is authentic. Loving is you. If it was your last day with your child, or if you knew it was going to be the last time you spoke, touched, or listened to your child, what would you say and how would you act? Would you be totally present, blocking out every distraction? Would you be unwavering, still, focused, peaceful, and loving? Would you be nitpicky, sarcastic, or judgmental?

Love is pure and is experienced in the present. Being present, being fully in tune, is where ease, peace, connection, and love reside.

If it was your last moment, wouldn't you give your child a hug and a kiss and show them you love them? Of course you would. So how do you know this is not your last moment? How do you know that tomorrow isn't your last day, or that this morning wasn't your last breakfast? Would that give you a different perspective on breakfast messes, insignificant crumbs, spilled orange juice, or messy jam faces? What if you lived each day to the fullest just because you honored the beauty and vulnerability of each passing day, and just because you have another day to spend with your kids? How blessed and grateful would you feel to be able to share in the experience with them?

By honoring each precious moment, how might you approach the screaming and running around the house, the noise, thrown objects, emotional outbursts, rage, tears, hitting, or messes around the house?

Do you yell, curse, swear, scold, punish, accuse, criticize, or abandon? Can you find within you presence, love, grace, peace, joy, acceptance, and enthusiasm?

Isn't this a truly conscious, awakened parent? To love no matter what, accept no matter what, and embrace no matter what? In some insanely perfect world, this has to be the true essence of parenting, since it is what you would do if you knew that today was your last day. It's the epitome of being love and giving love.

Be present, loving, surrendering, and joyful every moment of every day. Tell me one reason why someone cannot choose to have this as their standard of living. What if you could improve upon this way of being each day or week that passes? Before long, you would master this state of being. Screaming child in a mall? What are their needs and how do you love them more? Hissy fit in a restaurant? How do you love and accept them for them, model pure love, and offer your support and nurture them? The only way to feel great each day, energized, and joyful as a parent is to love.

How can you express, in your own unique style, your love and presence in the time you have with them? What is your most authentic style?

———————————

I cherish each and every moment.

three wise gifts

Children require so little. How much more money are you going to spend, knowing that your child will forget about the gift a week from now? How much more of your hard-earned salary will be spent on the illusion that your child needs more stuff and things to be happy?

Remember when you were a kid for a moment. How important was it that your refrigerator made ice cubes? How important was it that your cushions matched the furniture? How important was it that there were three cars in the driveway? How important was it that the windows were floor to ceiling?

The questions are not intended to imply that you should lower your standards of what you value, but don't confuse what your mind wants with what your kids want. It's important to acknowledge that it is our twisted concepts of idealism that convince us that our children need all kinds of things in order to be happy.

Kids gravitate to creativity and simplicity. They gravitate to learning and experiencing. They will not remember the life of accessories when they are older, just as you don't remember most of the material possessions you had when you were a child.

In fact, what you reminisce about are the times when you had very little, when resources were limited, when you made a fort out of tree branches or a boat out of a cardboard box. You don't reflect about all the things you had; you remember the joy you felt in what you created   ***Presence is a gift.*** out of nothing. Oh, of course, you will have had that special toy, doll, or bike that brings back a flood of wonderful memories, but how many "things" were really memorable?

There are three wise gifts that every parent must focus on: time, presence, and love.

They can be given each and every day, and monetarily they cost nothing.

Although time is a limiting concept, the reality is that we do have a certain length of stay on planet Earth in this particular body, with these particular people. We get one shot. Feel the vulnerability and urgency of that.

Presence is a gift. Presence allows you to tap into what's right in front of you. As with some meditative practices or work projects you become immersed in, presence overtakes any thoughts of the past or future. Presence means that you are living in the moment and can give of your whole self. When you are present, there is timelessness. This is where life is most abundant, joyful, loving, and grateful.

Love is our innate way of being. It's at the heart of who we are. We are capable of bringing this essence to any given moment. Love is surrender. Love is the ultimate experience between two people. Love is defenseless. Love is trust. Love is infinite and unconditioned. Love is the ultimate gift.

Parents stress about having to have a certain style of home, cars, or toys for their kids to grow up in or with. Kids don't care. They really don't. They only care about how safe and loved they feel. Anything beyond that is icing on the cake, and the extras won't be remembered anyway. They will, however, remember the relationships, the feeling of being cared for, and the feeling of being loved. They will remember joy, dancing, laughing, and fun. They will remember the meals, the attitudes, and the personalities around them; the freedom; the simplicity of being a child. This too is at the heart of what you crave as an adult.

Take a look at the photos of your kids, the smiles, the goofy looks, and realize those are the heartwarming, relevant moments.

Giving and receiving the three wise gifts is the ultimate human experience. Consider this combination the most valuable gift you can give to your children day in and day out.

The question is, can we learn to live outside the cultural expectations that our children need more stuff while still valuing the material world? What does your child truly need? What gifts are more valuable than these?

How could you package these gifts each day
to ensure you are meeting the needs of your children?

Diagram your week to see how you truly spend your time.
Are you content with what you see? If not, how can you resolve that?

I give all I can give.

there is no rationalizing

For a young child, there is no such thing as self-restraint or control. A child reacts simply because they are wired to. They don't have the capacity to think before they react. While children develop their emotions, they are developing the capacity to react. This is important for their survival. They don't have the brain development that enables rational thought to kick in. Rationalizing is not an option. To ask a child to think before they act is like trying to ask a beaver not to build its dam. They are not ready to override their emotions yet. To have the expectation that your child has the capacity to think before they act is causing both you and your child undue stress.

You know the saying "What were you thinking?" Simply, they weren't. Think about this. You still react from time to time, and you actually have the brain development to potentially override that. You as an adult have options, and yet you still lash out and react. How could you possibly expect your child not to react, lash out, hit, snap, yell, or scream?

Let your children react, and when they cool down, plant the seed for how you would like to see them respond in the future. It's not the time to punish them for reacting. That's like punishing you for being an adult. You're an adult. You aren't trying to be an adult. They aren't trying to be reactionary. They just are reactionary, until they aren't. You are there to plant the seeds for long-term behavior after they have cooled off.

Have a vision for what attributes you would like to instill and ones you feel are favorable to humanity: love, self-esteem, compassion, empathy, autonomy? Focus on those and reinforce those as seeds for a lifetime while honoring and embracing all their other parts.

How can you remind yourself to pause for a five-second breather the next time you are going to try to stop your child's natural reactions?

What parts of them are you having a difficult time accepting and loving?

I see the blessings in my child's emotions.

wholeness

I f you think you are going to raise happy kids who are not sad, good kids who are not bad, nice kids who are not mean, courageous kids who are not fearful, passive kids who are not aggressive, smart kids who are not stupid . . . good luck.

Our perception is that life is better or more balanced when it is one-sided. When life is only peaceful and not chaotic, and when there are happy times and not sad times. That expressing certain character traits is preferable than others. This is a great mistake.

There are two sides to all living things: the law of polarity. Everything in the universe has a polar opposite. There is day and night; build and destroy; fear and courage; success and failure; life and death; love and hate; clockwise and counterclockwise. Even the human being has polarity built within itself. You have been raised to think the world is supposed to be one-sided. Support with no challenge. Nice without mean. Kind without cruel. Happiness without sadness. Peace without anger.

The awakened parent accepts that both sides exist simultaneously. To fully embrace and accept that your child will do mean and caring acts, make smart and stupid choices, that they will be polite and rude: This is the test of love. This is awakened. To see both sides at the same time without judgment. Knowing that your child is not a one-sided but a two-sided child. The moment that you recognize and accept this, that your child has two sides to them, that is love. To attempt to wish for anything else is an illusion that creates suffering.

Surrendering to the perfection of both sides brings love. You see how the chaos in life is perfectly designed to bring balance and order to your world. It's when you realize and accept this perfect order that you can laugh at it. Let your children be whole by showing them that every part of them is acceptable and important.

How can you honor the importance of all traits
within you and your children?

Think of a time when you expressed anger.
What were the benefits to you of expressing this trait?

My family is whole and well.

surrender into love

There is no such thing as unconditional or conditional love. Love is just love. There are different expressions of love. Passionate love, compassionate love, empathetic love, maternal love. There are many different styles of expressing love. But love is love. Love is all-encompassing. Love is not lacking anything.

There is no void in love. You are either fully loving and being love, or you are having another agenda through the mind. Assume you are 100 percent love and own that as your truth. Then your only decision will be how to express that love.

Love is wholeness, which means that within love exists peace, rage, freedom, anger, curiosity, and all the other expressions. Love is everything, and it is the waking parent who can see through the illusions of everyday life and see how all the pleasures and pains alike make up love and wholeness.

What are your unique ways of expressing love?

How do you express love differently from other members of the family?

I express love in my own unique style.

4

transform

The Journey Continues

trans·form

to make a thorough or dramatic change
in the form, appearance, or character

To give ourselves the opportunity to transform, we must be willing to be vulnerable to the change. To be vulnerable to change means we have to do all the things we have talked about: become awake, be present, surrender, cease control, be curious, and be inspired.

In classic Buddhist teachings, "the beginner's mind" is a way to describe keeping one fresh, without clinging too far into the future or on a particular outcome, to stay vulnerable to change, and to stay in a state of everyday transformation. It's another way of staying present to opportunity for this transformation. If we can hold this space of transformation, then we hold the key to having our family life unfold with greater awareness, ease, acceptance, and excitement for each new day that comes. Each day really is a new day.

perfectly imperfect

erfectly imperfect implies that there is no right or wrong, only experience. That experience, no matter what it is, is perfect in that moment. As parents, we often criticize ourselves, get criticized, or criticize others for making decisions we could have or should have done differently. People choose what they choose, and you choose what you choose because it was perfect in that moment.

My wife uses a phrase to accept more of the "imperfect" present moment. She recites, "I'm supposed to be here right now." This allows her to stay present with what is, while remaining in an alert state to create something different when she's ready.

That does not mean that that decision will ever be perfect again. Trying to better the future through learning from experiences of the past is a great way to keep the mind thinking it has control. The parameters of the universe are too dynamic, and everything changes from moment to moment.

At every moment there are infinite possible choices. You can't cling to anything from the past, because the reason that decision was made was because it was perfect for that moment in time. Perfectly imperfect, embrace, and move on.

Instead of making decisions from fear or control, how can you place your focus so that *love* leads your decision-making?

Know that you have done the best you can in every moment, even if you feel you haven't; even if you feel it was reactive, angry, insulting, petty, argumentative, or any other reaction or response you deem less than your ideal. It was still the best you had at that moment. Then, one day, you look back and laugh. Better yet, why not laugh now?

As is time's way, everything changes in the next moment. The next decision will be perfect for that moment as the variables change. You may find yourself looking back again and saying "What was I doing?" Chances are you will think you are doing fantastic and look back in five years and say, "I can't believe I thought that was the right thing to do." Understand, it is an endless cycle, so surrender. "Why did I say that?" or "Why did I do that?" does not belong in your vocabulary anymore.

When you understand that everything really happens in a moment, what is there to change? You can't go back. What is done is done. Despite that, most of us say: "I will remember this decision I made so I can learn from it for the next time." You will repeat the experience as many times as you are supposed to, until you don't need to repeat it anymore and you make a new choice. And then, when you make a new choice, you may find it's not fitting either. Move on.

What steps can you take to surrender to being perfectly imperfect?

*Take a look at a stressful situation and identify five ways
that it is supporting you and five ways it is challenging you.
The balance of support and challenge is love. Take a good look
at how your life is loving you and is working to have you evolve.*

do your best,
and your best is good enough

U nderstand that in the moment, you are doing your best. It doesn't mean your awareness will not expand and you will not make different choices in a similar situation next time, but the next time will be perfect for that moment, not for previous moments. That's learning.

Experience the moment as your best moment based on what is available to you in terms of your energy, thoughts, emotions, and connection within you. If you chose to honor this concept, there will be no guilt, regret, sorrow, or feeling bad for the way things are. No second-guessing yourself. There would be no need for forgiveness, because you gave your absolute best in that moment with the exact resources that were available to you.

To understand this is to have empathy and compassion for who you were in that moment. It was your best because that was all you were capable of in that moment. If you said, "Well, I could have done more or I could have done better," that is not true. What is true is that if you could have, you would have. Therefore, what you did do, or say or not say, was the best you had for that moment in time. The fact that you could do better is the ego always wanting more and dreaming of a different reality and outcome.

Look back on a time in your life where you feel guilty or shameful. Look at the details of the event. How did you do your best in that moment?

Look at an unwanted circumstance you are experiencing right now. How are you doing your best to handle it?

one step at a time, one moment at a time

Each moment is in preparation for the next moment.

A marathon runner in training may be preparing for a race, but every run is practice and preparing for the next run in the training process. In fact, every step is preparation for the next step, every breath is in preparation for the next. And each breath is an experience in and of itself.

Just like the marathon runner trains one step at a time, so too do parents, one moment at a time. Knowing with clear awareness that the integrity of the moment, the attentiveness given to the moment, is also preparation for the future.

When you are with your child, this is the moment. This is the one breath. It is the moment to experience. One hug, one kiss, one smile, one nudge, one encouragement after the other is preparing for the next moment, which will prepare for future moments when they are twenty, thirty, forty, and so on. The most important thing you can focus on is experiencing one moment at a time.

What does taking life one breath, one step at a time mean to you?

What are the steps you can take to surrender to each moment so you can be present with those around you?

acknowledgments

To my mother, Loretta. You have encouraged me, guided me, loved me, and always made me feel like I had more than enough. I love you more than words can express. Thank you so much for all of your support.

To my dad, Larry. I know the threads of our souls are always connected and that my suffering was your suffering, and my victories were your victories. I know you did your best, and that is more than enough for me.

To my sister, Leanne. What's life without a pair of opposites? Without you, there is no me. So thank you for giving me the experiences that helped to shape my life.

I want to thank all the hundreds of colleagues and mentors along the way. There are way too many to mention, and I thank all of you for your guidance and mentorship.

I want to send a special thank-you to Dr. Donny Epstein, whose genius has allowed me to provide such a unique service to humanity while assisting in my continued waking.

To Dr. John Demartini, who provided me with the tools, knowledge, and skill set to consistently remember who I am, why I'm here, and what I'm made of.

To Dr. Gilles LaMarche, for his patience, trust, and faith in me to write and follow my dreams.

A special thank-you to Dr. Daniel Chenier and Dr. Aaron Wilkerson. I cherish our friendship.

Editors at Penguin, including Marian Lizzi, as well as assistance from Loretta Fonso, Gilles LaMarche, Lea Fonso: thank you for all the time and effort you put in to help take my insights and put them in a reader-friendly format.

Dr. Steven Fonso was born and raised in Thunder Bay, Canada, where at an early age he showed the signs of great leadership. Through his athletics and in school settings, there seemed to be this natural tendency to be a voice of inspiration and encouragement. This desire to help encourage people to be better led him to pursue a profession in chiropractic—a profession designed to assist humanity through maximizing their human potential. During school and after graduation, his emphasis of study was philosophy, health, human potential, personal development, consciousness, and spirituality. In 2004 he opened his first private practice, helping thousands to become healthier and more vital. He has worked with people challenged with anxiety, depression, drug addictions, and chronic pain. He has also worked with Olympic athletes, business entrepreneurs, and families. With a keen desire for personal mastery combined with an appetite to serve others, in 2009 he created Veressent Life, an educational organization designed to help people begin their journey with the ultimate focus: a life dedicated to living in one's authentic, core nature. He knew that when people are living in their natural states, there is connection, peace, love, gratitude, and inspiration. He hosts seminars, workshops, and retreats to provide people with the experience and education needed to further their connection to their core essence and to live an inspired life. He now teaches parents, educators, and team leaders on how to best manage their inner state while working with young children and how to get the most out of the children's potential, as well as providing strategies to overcome the challenging stresses of everyday life. Dr. Fonso runs online education courses and offers memberships to support the essence of his work, with a special emphasis on health and healing, personal and relationship mastery, and strategies to maximize the wellness of the family dynamic. Dr. Fonso lives with his beautiful wife, Lea, and their three children.

For more information, questions, or inquiries, visit his website at stevenfonso.com.